Praise for *Marriage Minded:*
*An A to Z Dating Guide*

"*Marriage Minded* is the most important book to come out on dating and marriage and long overdue. It addresses so many different aspects of dating and marriage in a language that is elegant yet so relevant. I wish it would be required reading for college students for its sage advice and common-sense coaching."
—SARAH KARMELY, marriage educator, marriage counselor, and author of *Words to Hear with Your Heart* and *Stories to Hear with Your Heart*

"As an attorney/mediator who has helped couples unhitch for thirty years, I've seen how most people don't have the skills to maintain a long-lasting, loving marriage. In *Marriage Minded*, Marcia Naomi Berger, an expert therapist, gives women excellent advice, helpful examples, and important steps to becoming happily married."
—MARI FRANK, ESQ., coauthor of *Fighting for Love: Turn Conflict Into Intimacy—A Couple's Guide*

"*Marriage Minded* begins with self-understanding, the first step for anyone seeking a fulfilling, lasting union. You'll gain intelligent, practical approaches for dating, committing, and staying happily married. The book is research-based yet practical and fun to read."
—SUSAN PAGE, author of *If I'm So Wonderful, Why Am I Still Single?*

"For women hoping to settle down with a man, this balanced book offers down-to-earth guidance in an easy-to-read, A-to-Z format. Berger's wise advice will help build a healthy relationship."
—MATTHEW D. JOHNSON, PhD, professor of psychology at Binghamton University and author of *Great Myths of Intimate Relationships: Dating, Sex, and Marriage*

# Marriage Minded

An A *to* Z
Dating Guide
*for* Lasting
Love

Marcia Naomi Berger, LCSW

SHE WRITES PRESS

Published 2021
Printed in the United States of America
Print ISBN: 978-1-64742-179-3
E-ISBN: 978-1-64742-180-9
Library of Congress Control Number: 2021908664

For information, address:
She Writes Press
1569 Solano Ave #546
Berkeley, CA 94707

Illustrations by Erica Dallman
Interior design by Tabitha Lahr

She Writes Press is a division of SparkPoint Studio, LLC.

*In loving memory of*
*Mollie Herman Fisch Goldfarb, my mother,*
*who showed you can find lasting love later in life*

# CONTENTS

# S is for

## Committing

# T is for

# Z is for

# Introduction

Do you long for a soul mate? You're not alone. It's human nature to want a life partner. Yet because many unions don't last these days, we may hope to say "I do" but fear disappointment. I was like this. I had avoided commitment for so long that at my wedding thirty-three years ago, a friend quipped, "It's the end of an era."

When I told my mother I was engaged, she said, "It's a miracle." She expected me to stay single and avoid the heartbreak she'd suffered. My father divorced her when I was thirteen. "I gave him the best years of my life," she said. When she knew I was seeing someone, she'd ask, "Is he still nice?" meaning he'd disappoint me sooner or later.

So I'd stopped telling her about men in my life. As far as she knew, I hadn't had a date in ten years. "Get a dog," she once said. "Anything to cuddle with." No wonder my news surprised her.

I believe in marriage.

Like many adult children of divorce, I was conflicted about marrying. I'd trusted that my parents would stay together. Yet I still longed to marry. Cinderella married her perfect prince. So did heroines of romantic novels and movies. Why shouldn't I find mine and then live effortlessly happily ever after? My prince was out there somewhere. We just hadn't found each other yet.

A happily married coworker told me when we were both in our twenties: "You don't marry a prince. You make him one." Great advice, though it took me a very long time to implement it. I am grateful to her and other mentors.

Crazy-in-love is a fantasy, but "in love" can be real. As Mignon McLaughlin says. "A successful marriage requires falling in love many times, always with the same person." Fondness needs to be there for this to happen, as does the sort of thoughtfulness that fosters it, which is what happens when we respect each other's wishes and needs.

You too can find your prince. Sometimes you may view him as perfect, although he's undoubtedly a diamond in the rough. Occasionally, you might see a frog. But if you choose your spouse wisely and apply the knowledge in this book, you'll create your real-life type of happily ever after.

Ample research confirms that marriage is good for us. Marriage has challenges and also great rewards. People in a satisfying marriage have more sex, better sleep, and better mental and physical health. But a marriage that is not healthy will negatively affect one's well-being. By choosing a partner wisely, gaining knowledge about creating a gratifying marriage, and applying this information, you can succeed.

To prepare you for a lasting, fulfilling union, *Marriage Minded* has four sections: (1) Overcoming Obstacles, (2) Dating, (3) Committing, and (4) Marriage.

Societal pressure to marry has decreased. Economic incentives are less relevant. So why marry? New, yet often unconscious, reasons exist for tying the knot. Most of us long for a lasting union that fulfills us emotionally and spiritually, as well as physically and materially. This book tells how to create such a marriage.

Not all women who hope to marry will say so when cynics are stating marriage is obsolete. Some women don't speak about their desire because they fear people will view them as desperate.

A mother told me that her daughter, Emily, forty-six, wasn't interested in marriage. That's what Emily told her. Then I met Emily, an attractive public relations executive with a bright smile. Privately, she looked me in the eye and said, "I want to get married. My friends do too."

Susan, twenty-six, with a four-year-old daughter, said: "My life is fine." Yet in moments of vulnerability, she asks, "Why can't I meet a great man who accepts me, really cares for me, and wants to be with me for life?"

Beth, sixty-eight, gave up on finding a partner after her second divorce twenty years ago. Recently, she confided, "I want to get married. But I'm afraid of the 'meet market' (or meat market, as some people think of it) and being rejected if I put myself out there. Can you help me?"

As a clinical social worker, psychotherapist, and Marry with Confidence workshop leader, I've seen people of all ages create great marriages. My clients have been benefiting from the principles and techniques in this book for over thirty-five years. And in my own life, I practice what I preach.

Many women in their twenties and early thirties are eager to wed and have children. Others want to establish their careers first, which is another reason later marriages are more common. Plenty of women in their forties to seventies and beyond are marrying for the first time, or again.

Whether you want to marry and start or blend a family or are seeking a partner later in life, this book can guide you. It includes stories of how many women overcame obstacles and gained beautiful, lasting marriages. Marriage is here to stay.

My mother loved me. She warned me about who not to marry. Doctors were too stuck up, lawyers argued too much, and of course, drinkers and gamblers were to be avoided. (Good thing accountants weren't on her reject list because I married one.)

Yet her story has a happy ending. At a later age, my mother found love. She spent the last eight years of her life married to a wonderful man who cherished her—another miracle.

Every good marriage is a miracle, and you can create one. I've written *Marriage Minded* with single women in mind, yet much of its A to Z advice can guide anyone toward relationship success.

# Overcoming Obstacles

*Always measure an obstacle next
to the size of the dream you're pursuing.*
—Bill Vaughan

 **is for**

○ **Ambivalence**
○ **Anxiety**
○ **Attitude**
○ **Awareness**
○ **Awesome**

## AMBIVALENCE

Ambivalence is normal. In many situations, a part of us wants to do something, and another part of us fears to do it. "It" could be making a phone call or a purchase, accepting a job, or marrying someone.

If you've wanted to get married for a long time but for some reason it hasn't happened, you may be ambivalent.

Shari met men effortlessly. She thought it was just luck that she hadn't met the right one. Over the years, Michael, her best friend's husband, had heard her complain about one man after another with whom she'd been romantically involved. When she was about to gripe about the latest, Michael chimed in, imitating her: "I like him a lot, but he doesn't want to get serious."

*Ouch!* Shari felt embarrassed; he'd exposed her pattern. Quickly, she put it out of her mind.

Eventually, Shari realized that she'd been sabotaging herself by continuing to relate to men who didn't want marriage. That was how she'd been acting out her ambivalence.

Shari had grown up without seeing a good marriage. During her adolescence, after her parents divorced, her mother often told her mournfully, "He left me for that woman." Unconsciously, Shari believed that sooner or later, a husband would break her heart. So she found fault with any marriage-minded man who liked her and pined after the other sort.

Eventually, Shari gained self-understanding and confidence that she could succeed in marriage. Long after Michael had metaphorically hit her over the head with her self-defeating pattern, she finally reversed it, with the help of a good therapist. She married a wonderful man.

Knowledge is power. So recognize your ambivalence if it's there. Uncover your hopes and also your fears. Gain information about how to date successfully and how to create a lasting, fulfilling marriage.

# ANXIETY

It's natural to feel anxious about making a significant life change. Ask yourself, "What am I afraid of?" Discussing and perhaps writing out your fears can be your first step to getting past them.

Many people who lacked role models for an excellent lifelong union fear that they'll fail at marriage. Such people may have parents who either divorced or stayed together unhappily while they were growing up.

Dina thought getting married meant she'd have to eat all her meals with a husband and always sleep together in the same bed. She craved companionship but often liked having her own space. Dina feared marriage would be too confining. A happily married friend told her that spouses don't usually eat all of their meals together, and many couples have separate beds. For Dina, realizing she could negotiate to meet her needs helped her feel more confident about marrying.

# ATTITUDE

*Everything can be taken from a man but one thing: the last of human freedoms—to choose one's attitude in any given set of circumstances, to choose one's own way.*
—VIKTOR E. FRANKL

Are you feeling confident or unsure about marrying? Women in my Marry with Confidence workshops have expressed these attitudes:

- All the good men are married.
- There aren't enough single men in my area.
- Men my age want a much younger woman.
- Men want a thinner woman.
- I'm afraid of getting into a bad marriage.
- I'm too flawed to create a good marriage.

Are you telling yourself any of these things? If yes, you can do some rethinking. Self-awareness is the first step toward gaining a positive, realistic attitude.

Beliefs can create self-fulfilling prophecies. If you think that all the good men have been taken, you may ignore fine men or

## Attitude Adjustment

Before         After

reject them for senseless reasons. You're less likely to notice such men; they're beneath your radar.

If you're sending yourself negative messages, examine them. Here's how:

- *All the good men are married.*

  All the good men are not married. You may be assuming that they are all married as a way to avoid facing your ambivalence about marrying.

- *There aren't enough single men in my area.*

  If there is a lack of eligible men in your location, options still exist. Julie was thirty-two and marriage minded. Like me, she was living in Marin County, California, a suburban area filled with many married folks and relatively few single men. But she knew where to find men.

  Julie drove over an hour to singles events in Silicon Valley, loaded with single men working in computer-related industries. She met her husband at one. They've been married for thirty-two years. When I met my husband, he too lived in Silicon Valley. We met at a singles gathering in San Francisco.

  Just because there may be relatively few available men in your area doesn't mean that you can't marry one of them. As my mother, of blessed memory, used to say, "It only takes one!"

  These days, with all the available online dating sites, it's easier than ever to meet a marriage-minded man, regardless of where you live.

- *Men my age want a much younger woman.*

  Forget about men who want a trophy wife. Instead, look for someone mature enough to relate to you as an equal. You'll be happier with a partner with good character traits, similar values, and enough common interests. Such men want a best friend to connect with emotionally and spiritually. They do notice appearance first, so besides letting your inner self shine, of course, you'll want to keep looking your best.

- ### *Men want a thinner woman.*

  Some men dwell on superficial characteristics, like height, weight, or income. You'll be much happier with someone who treasures your essence. If you value your unique individuality, you are likely to attract a man who recognizes your worth. Another memorable quote from my mother is about zaftig (a Yiddish word meaning plump or full-figured) women: "Some men like to get lost in the folds."

- ### *I'm afraid of getting into a bad marriage.*

  The fear of having an unhappy marriage must be a common one. Divorce rates are cited at about 50 percent for first marriages and even higher for subsequent ones. Why is this happening?

  Some marriages don't last because the partners were initially attracted but not compatible for the long haul. Many unions fail because spouses have not learned how to communicate well. Others don't succeed because they committed after not having paid attention to red flags.

  Knowledge is power. By gaining self-awareness, learning what qualities you need in a marriage partner, and growing your communication skills, you'll be on your way to creating a fulfilling, lifelong marriage.

  You can succeed in marriage by choosing your partner wisely and learning how to relate successfully in dating and marriage. By applying this book's information, you'll gain the marriage you've always wanted—one that fulfills you emotionally and spiritually, as well as physically and materially.

- *I'm too flawed to create a good marriage.*
So maybe you're feeling disadvantaged because you're a little neurotic or perceive some other imperfection you think could block you from getting to happily ever after. Regardless of outward appearances, everyone has insecurities, eccentricities, hot buttons related to "unfinished business" from childhood, or something else.

This dialogue from the 1976 movie *Rocky* says it well about "gaps":

> **Paulie:** [talking about Adrian] You like her?
> **Rocky:** Sure, I like her.
> **Paulie:** What's the attraction?
> **Rocky:** I dunno . . . she fills gaps.
> **Paulie:** What's gaps?
> **Rocky:** I dunno, she's got gaps, I got gaps, together we fill gaps.

Of course, we can—and should—do our best to grow toward our best selves. But there will always be gaps. Guess what! In a good marriage, you can still be neurotic after tying the knot. Your husband will keep loving you, the whole package, and stick around for the long haul. And you should expect to reciprocate.

Before marriage, many of us act out our issues, like fear of abandonment, sensitivity to criticism, concern about body image, or some other insecurity, with men in our lives temporarily. After marriage, we still do our "stuff," but with the same person again and again because he sticks around and fills gaps!

## Developing an Optimistic Mindset

It would not be realistic to say marriage success is as easy as ABC. If you have a long-established pessimistic pattern about marriage, don't expect to change your attitude overnight. But if you sincerely want to overcome this obstacle and apply this book's A to Z information that fits for you, you can expect to succeed.

# AWARENESS

Awareness is the key to learning. It leads to change because once we are aware, we can make choices. So be curious enough to ask yourself: "Do I have a pattern, a habitual way of behaving that may be holding me back from dating or marrying?" (See page 145 for Self-Awareness.)

*Exercise*

Answering these questions can help you gain awareness of your attitude toward marriage and decide whether you want to change it:

- How and where do you meet men?
- Do you avoid opportunities for meeting men? If yes, why? What's holding you back?
- Do you stay in a relationship with a man who is not interested in commitment?
- Do you reject men who are marriage minded by finding fault with each one?

# AWESOME

*Birth is G-d saying you matter.*
—Menachem Mendel Schneerson,
the Lubavitcher Rebbe

Yes, you are awesome! Celebrate your aliveness and your uniqueness, and others will recognize it too.

You were put here on earth to fulfill a purpose that is uniquely yours. So keep using your intelligence, resourcefulness, and creativity to do whatever you need to do as part of a meaningful life. You *can* make your dreams come true!

# Dating

 **is for**

- ○ Balance
- ○ Be Aware
- ○ Be Yourself
- ○ Boundaries

## BALANCE

By taking good care of the physical, spiritual, social, and psychological aspects of our lives while dating, we're likely to relax, stay attractive, and smoothly handle whatever comes up.

Doing the suggested exercise based on the chart on the next page, you may decide to adjust the amount of time or energy you're now spending in each of these four dimensions: Biological/Physical, Psychological, Social, and Spiritual.

# Live the life you love; love the life you live!

## *Self-Care Grid[1]*

### Biological/Physical

- Exercise
- Diet
- Rest
- Toxic substances
- Good medical care
- Financial wellness

### Psychological

- Stress
- A full range of emotions
- A sense of purpose
- Positive thinking
  (Core issues: self-defeating patterns of behavior that continue to sabotage your life. It's essential to have someone to give you feedback, to call you on your "stuff.")

### Social

- Friends—people who lift you or hold you back
- Reciprocal love—needing someone to hold you and say you're okay
- Intimacy
- Support
- Commitment
- Fun
- Solitude—Are you okay with being alone with yourself?

### Spiritual

- Religious honesty
- Spiritual practice
- Meaning
- Integrity
- Continuous growth in knowledge and practice

The goal is to get all areas in balance. Look for both quantity and proportion. Score yourself for each dimension, allowing up to twenty-five points for each box. Add the scores for each box to get your total score. Then draw four labeled circles (as per grid labels), and stack them like a snowman (or snowwoman). Size each circle according to your score in each box.

## Is your life balanced enough?

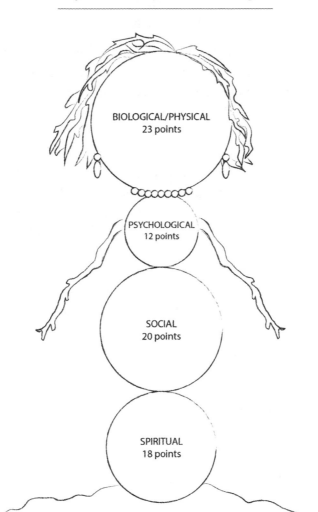

BIOLOGICAL/PHYSICAL
23 points

PSYCHOLOGICAL
12 points

SOCIAL
20 points

SPIRITUAL
18 points

Decide on which area(s) you need to invest more energy into to become more balanced. If you're serious about doing this, decide how you will do so and by what date. If applicable, ask a buddy to help you achieve this goal so you'll have the support of someone to whom you'll be accountable. Also, make sure that you know why you are making the change, not just to get married but to be consistent with your values.

# BE AWARE

What are you looking for in a marriage partner? The exercises under the Lists entry, page 79, ask you to identify the traits you want or need in your future marriage partner. Your list is likely to remain in your subconscious and help you attract a man who's right for you.

It took me some time to become aware of my real wants and needs. When I was dating and hoping to marry, men like Roger entranced me. We had common interests, similar backgrounds, and sparkling conversation. He was smart and witty, and the chemistry—wow! His attentiveness thrilled me. When we first met, I told Roger I liked William Turner's misty paintings of seas, skies, and ships. On our first date, he gave me a coffee table book about Turner's art and life.

*He's perfect*, I thought, still infatuated on our second date. We took a walk along a creek with my dog, Amie, a sweet basenji mix. And then came the first red flag: Roger asked, "Doesn't a dog tie you down?"

I wanted marriage and motherhood. But I ignored that signal and a couple of other caution signs. Like how Roger explained his divorce after six months of marriage: "She took up too much closet space." He wasn't joking.

I'm skeptical about people who blame their divorce entirely on their former spouse or cite a minor flaw of an ex-spouse to explain a breakup. But Roger was just so sweet that after briefly sensing that I should be wary, I put my blinders back on. We enjoyed dinner that night at a cozy French restaurant.

For our third date, Roger suggested a hike with the singles group we both belonged to. I said okay, although he'd be near the front and I'd be bringing up the rear, given our different abilities. My friend Jackie, hiking by my side, asked, "If Roger's interested in you, why is he asking you to go on a singles hike?" I wondered too, but I shoved down the queasy feeling in my gut.

After the hike, Roger and I had dinner at the same French restaurant. Back at my place, he seemed so smitten during our long goodnight hug that I softly asked when I'd hear from him again. He tensed up. I felt an urge to test him. "How about Tuesday or Wednesday? Will you call me then?" I asked gently.

He backed away. "I don't like pressure," he said.

I felt awful; I sensed it was over. But by the following evening, something clicked for me. I used to try to hold on to going-nowhere relationships and try to get the guy back if he seemed to be losing interest in me. But Roger had nearly screamed, "I don't want marriage! I don't want kids!" This time I realized he wasn't for me.

Wanting closure, I phoned him. I said I'd noticed a pattern: he would create distance when we seemed to be getting close. I said, "This isn't working for me." After a few moments of what I sensed was stunned silence on his part, he said, "Can we still be friends?" I said, "Of course," understanding this meant if our paths crossed, we'd be cordial and not bad-mouth each other.

If he was shocked by my call, I was too. I had stated my boundary: no more casual relationships! I'd allow only marriage-minded men into my life.

By being aware of what you need in a partner and knowing your excellent qualities that a potential husband is likely to appreciate, you're on your way to a lasting, fulfilling relationship.

**Her mind is on marriage-minded men.**

# BE YOURSELF

*"Be yourself; everyone else is already taken."*
—OSCAR WILDE

If you're content with who you are, your fine qualities will appear naturally. You'll be appreciated for your presence. Also, for your smile, insights, companionship, vibrancy, sensitivity, confidence, drive, intelligence, curiosity, ability to listen, and so on.

Appreciate yourself. Any woman who expects to blossom only after Prince Charming sweeps her off into a blissful life is misleading herself.

Do not try to squeeze yourself into a mold that fits a man's expectation—unless you are ready to stifle your soul. In order to relate authentically to another person, we must allow our true selves to show. If you're truly comfortable with who you are—with your values, interests, and personal traits—you won't feel a need to be a people pleaser and forget who you really are.

When you develop an accepting, honest relationship with yourself, your glow will attract the best kinds of men *for you*. In being yourself, you give a unique, precious gift to others. And you will enjoy dating much more after you become your own best friend.

# BOUNDARIES

Just because someone is attentive or says he loves you, that doesn't signal whether he's right for you in the long term. Imagine a fence around your personal space. In front of it is a "Keep Out" sign that applies to men who don't belong in your life. The fence is your boundary. It protects you from wasting time and energy you should save for a good potential husband.

As explained in Be Aware, page 12, it's vital to notice the signals a man sends about his readiness for marriage. By heeding red flags, you can avoid involvement with someone whose goal doesn't match yours, no matter how charming he might be.

# C is for

- Character
- Chemistry
- Choose
- Clarity
- Comfort Zone
- Communication
- Curiosity

## CHARACTER

Maybe he looks like George Clooney, Brad Pitt, or your favorite heartthrob. He may also be brilliant, successful, and fun. But character is too crucial to ignore, no matter how besotted you may feel.

Your chances of gaining a lasting, fulfilling marriage will be greatly enhanced if you

- identify the character traits you need in a husband;
- recognize that traits such as empathy, loyalty, respect, kindness, patience, and self-acceptance are essential for long-term compatibility;
- get to know him well enough over time to assess objectively whether he has the traits you need; and

16

- realize that character improvement is a lifelong challenge for all of us, yet you deserve someone with essential good qualities.

# CHEMISTRY

Chemistry counts, but how much? When it comes to a romantic relationship, *chemistry* is a loaded word. Does one of these beliefs pop into your mind when you hear it?

- For a good relationship, chemistry needs to exist right away.
- Chemistry might not be felt initially but can develop later.
- Love at first sight, or a variation of this, predicts a good long-term relationship.
- Chemistry can come and go, depending on other factors.
- Chemistry is not necessary for a good marriage.
- Chemistry can attract you to the "wrong" person.

Let's take a closer look at each of these ideas about chemistry.

- *For a good relationship, chemistry needs to exist right away.*
**False.** Chemistry does not need to be there right away. As sex experts William Masters and Virginia Johnson state, the most important sexual organ is between the ears. When you first meet someone, you may feel attracted right away because, perhaps unconsciously, he or she reminds you of someone you love or admire.

But your initial attraction does not predict the future. After getting to know the person better, you may find that he's too critical, demanding, or untrustworthy, or that he doesn't share values you hold dear.

- *Chemistry might not be felt initially but can develop later.*
**True.** Here's an example of a relationship in which a woman didn't experience chemistry initially but later did:

When Jen met Peter at a singles' gathering, she enjoyed talking with him. *He's much too young for me*, she thought, *but he's nice, like a sweet younger brother*. When he asked her out, she said yes. She soon learned that he wasn't as young as she'd thought. Once she realized this, chemistry developed. They married a year later.

Another reason you may not feel chemistry on first meeting someone is that you're stressed. Work, family, or another concern might preoccupy you. But later, when you're relaxed, an attraction might develop.

It can take time for chemistry to happen. So if you feel compatible and not repelled by someone, don't give up too soon. A mutual attraction may develop over time as you get to know each other. Full-blown shivers-down-the-spine love is probably a short-lived infatuation. The potential for lasting love exists when the two of you enjoy each other's company and look forward to spending time together and conversing. And if these basics are missing, it's okay to move on after a couple of dates. Trust your gut to tell you who you want to keep in your life, at least for now.

True love will develop more deeply during a good marriage, as explained in the Love entry, page 82.

- *Love at first sight, or a variation of this, predicts a good long-term relationship.*

**False.** Not usually. Some couples fall in love instantly, then quickly marry, and it works out well. These are the lucky ones, probably because they have enough shared values and interests and desirable character traits that stand the test of time.

Love at first sight is *not* an accurate predictor of relationship success. A thirteen-year longitudinal study by Tom Huston at the University of Texas at Austin (Huston et al., 2001) found that couples with longer courtships who learn about each other's positive traits and weaknesses were more likely to remain happily married over time. Couples with passionate courtships that quickly resulted in marriage soon grew dissatisfied and were more likely to divorce within seven years.[1]

• *Chemistry can come and go, depending on other factors.*
**True.** The "in love" feelings come and go, based on the other person's behavior and our internal state of mind at the moment.

• *Chemistry is not necessary for a good marriage.*
**False.** There needs to be some attraction. If no spark is present after a few dates, it's time to move on. Someone might be nice, sweet, and have integrity, but if no attraction develops, that person may become an excellent spouse—for someone else.

• *Chemistry can attract you to the "wrong" person.*
**True.** Do you want marriage, but you're attracted to people who won't commit? If so, you might be acting out an internal conflict experienced by many. Part of you longs for commitment; another part fears it won't work out. Unconsciously, you play it safe by being attracted only to people who want a casual relationship. By gaining self-awareness and skills for creating a successful marriage, you can move past this conflict and allow chemistry to happen with the right person.

# CHOOSE

Choose wisely. It's not a matter of finding the right guy, and the magic should happen. It's more about finding someone with qualities you value who's willing to work with you when issues arise—and they will.

Take your time getting to know him without letting your emotions take over. You're more likely to make a wise choice for a lifetime partner if you keep your head clear while getting to know him.

# CLARITY

Are you clear about

- the traits you need in a husband?
- your ability to succeed in marriage?
- what you have to offer in marriage?
- how to know when to stay in or end a relationship?
- whether you genuinely want marriage?

## Traits You Need in a Husband

By clarifying the qualities you value in a husband, you are likely to choose wisely. (See Lists, page 79.) Think through your list carefully. Replace superficial traits, such as hair color, height, or occupation, with more important ones. You're more likely to stay happily married to someone who may lack an unessential trait but possesses more important ones—like similar values, excellent character traits, and the ability to support and appreciate your interests, even when he doesn't share them.

## Your Ability to Succeed

Many of us lack confidence in our ability to succeed in marriage. When we hear the dismal divorce statistics, why wouldn't we be afraid to commit, especially if we've already divorced or our parents have?

Some fear that they'll fail at marriage because they lack self-esteem or feel too flawed.

Knowledge is power. You *can* succeed by learning how. You can learn to create a lasting, fulfilling marriage by applying the information in this book and others (see Reading List, page 221).

## What You Have to Offer

Later, you'll be asked to note qualities in yourself that a potential husband is likely to appreciate (See Lists, page 79). Are you caring and trustworthy? Good at listening? Creative? Do you have a good sense of humor? Recognizing that you have much to offer will increase your self-confidence and make you shine. Your aura will attract a good potential husband.

## Knowing When to Stay in or End a Relationship

If you're dating with marriage in mind, you'll want to find out soon if he's like-minded. Your time is too precious to spend with someone who wants a different type of relationship.

## Do You Genuinely Want Marriage?

Some women say they want marriage but have not thought through their mixed feelings. When Karen asked for a therapy session with me, she said she wanted to get past whatever was getting in her way of marrying. Slim, attractive, and in her early forties, she has a successful career. Her first marriage ended in divorce. Since then, she'd been in several uncommitted relationships. She was currently dating and having sex with a man she liked, although he'd made it clear that he didn't want marriage. During our first session, she said she would be taking a vacation with him next month.

"If you want to get married, why are you still seeing him?" I asked. She said she'd need to think about that. She canceled what would have been her second session, saying she realized she didn't want to get married.

No law says you have to marry. It's a very personal decision and an important one to gain clarity about.

# COMFORT ZONE

Do you feel cynical about marriage? Are you spending time with friends who feel the same way because you're comfortable with people who share your view, like "birds of a feather who flock together"?

If you honestly long for marriage, don't let your comfort zone hold you back. Spend less time with naysayers. Get to know people in successful relationships. They can inspire you and serve as role models. Help yourself to a realistic, constructive, optimistic outlook.

# COMMUNICATION

*The single biggest problem in communication*
*is the illusion that it has taken place.*
—George Bernard Shaw

We might think that our spoken words send the message people take in. Yet studies by Albert Mehrabian, PhD, and his colleagues confirm the truth of the familiar maxim "It's not what you say; it's how you say it."[2]

Here is what they found regarding how much of the message received by the listener is based on the sender's words, voice, and body language in personal communications:

- spoken words: 7%
- voice tone: 38%
- body language: 55%

Voice tone includes volume and inflection. Examples of body language include eye contact, facial expression, body position (such as facing toward or turned away from the other person, arms open or crossed), and posture. So, especially during a meaningful conversation, be aware of your voice tone and body language, as well as the words you say.

Remember to smile when you express appreciation. Look in the eye of the person with whom you want to connect. Use a friendly, soft voice if you would like to come across as accepting and compassionate, even when discussing a problem or challenge.

## The Gift of Silence

Saying nothing can be the most effective form of communication when done sensitively, especially when the other person needs to feel heard and understood. Listening with complete concentration, not injecting your thoughts and feelings into the moment, can be a treasured gift.

When someone asks for your advice or opinion, it's okay to give it. But if you don't know if your viewpoint is wanted, you can ask, "Do you want to hear my thoughts?" Your feedback might be helpful—if desired.

Many of us find that venting helps us process our thoughts and feelings. When we're heard with no interruptions, a solution often arises from within, as if by magic. Certainly, there's a time for words. Yet silence is often both welcome and powerful.

Finally, the most important communication consists of the messages we tell ourselves. (See Self-Talk, page 149.)

# CURIOSITY

*Wisdom begins in wonder.*

—SOCRATES

By showing curiosity, you communicate care and interest. So when you are wondering about a man's thoughts and feelings, let him know. You might ask how he chose his occupation and what he likes about it. What drew him to live where he does? What does he do for fun? These are a few examples of suitable first date getting-to-know-you questions.

Anything you're interested in knowing is okay to ask him about, as long as you're respecting his privacy. A sensitive topic like why he got divorced could be off-putting on a first or second date, but you will want to ask reasonably soon. How he responds may show whether he recognizes his role in the breakup and if he's learned from the experience.

## Expressing Curiosity Clears Up Confusion

Cindy was confused by Jeff's phone call. They'd been going out for a couple of months, and now he said he was planning to go to a New Year's Eve party near where he lived. "It would be a long drive for you, so I don't suppose you'd want to come," he said.

No, she didn't want to make the hour-long trip. But didn't Jeff wish to come to see her on New Year's Eve? Had he lost interest in her, or what?

After stewing a bit, Cindy phoned Jeff and said, "I'm wondering why you're not asking me out for New Year's Eve." He said he'd like to be with her but didn't want to drive home late at night with the threat of drunk drivers on the road. Cindy, who had decided against sex in an uncommitted relationship, suggested that he sleep on the sofa bed in her living room, which he did.

Cindy hoped to marry and be a stay-at-home mom for some time after babies came along. She was curious: would Jeff be able to support a wife and family financially?

Jeff was working only two days a week, which barely earned him enough to support himself but allowed him lots of gym and hiking time. Cindy said, "You've said that you want to marry and have children, but how can you support a family when you're working only two days a week?" Jeff said that his situation was temporary. He was taking it easy for a while after having left a demanding job he'd held for nine years. Reassured, Cindy was glad that she'd asked.

## Cultivate an Accepting Spirit

Your curiosity is healthy when your questions aren't meant to bait or criticize him. Ask and listen with an accepting spirit. You intend to understand, not to judge.

Be curious about yourself too, and be accepting of what you discover. According to psychiatrist Judson Brewer, being curious about what you're doing, why you're choosing to do it, and what else you might decide to do can lead to long-term change.[3]

# D is for

- ○ Deal Breaker
- ○ Dignity
- ○ Diligence

## DEAL BREAKER

Mary Ellen, a committed Catholic, loved Jack and wanted to marry him until not-so-religious Jack said no to a Catholic wedding. Mary Ellen knew what she needed. His refusal was a deal breaker, so they broke up. Thirteen days later, Jack agreed to tie the knot her way with a Catholic wedding. They've now been happily married for over forty years.

Knowing where to draw the line is crucial. Whether you want or don't want children, stepchildren, a pet, a particular lifestyle, religious observance, or something else, make sure to find out sooner rather than later whether a potential spouse is like-minded.

If you want a good marriage, why waste precious dating time on someone whose vision of a happy life differs significantly from yours?

## Not Spotting a Deal Breaker Is Risky

Lila knew she wanted children, and Paul always said he didn't. She thought he'd eventually change his mind. Ten years into their relationship, they became engaged. Then he broke it off. He said it wouldn't work because he didn't want to be a parent. That's when Lila, thirty-two, came to see me for therapy.

What if Lila had recognized that this deal breaker existed when Paul first told her he didn't want children? Instead of needing to grieve over the breakup and worry about her biological clock ticking, Lila might well have met and married someone who shared her goal.

So do ask yourself what really matters to you. Like Mary Ellen did about her wedding, be ready to end a relationship that will result in your feeling shortchanged or big-time resentful. Do make sure to know the difference between a want and a need. (See Lists, page 79.) No one gets everything they *want*, so don't expect perfection. A deal breaker exists only when something that you genuinely *need* for your happiness in life is missing.

# DIGNITY

Dating, like a job interview, can feel stressful. We want to make a good impression, and we may feel unsure about succeeding. Regardless of feelings of self-doubt that may crop up, your default position should be, "I feel good about myself. I'll marry someone who treasures me, regardless of how this date turns out." Maintaining your dignity is vital before and after marriage. Here are a few dos and don'ts on this subject:

## Do

- stay aware of and respect your wants and needs;
- maintain your boundaries regarding acceptable behavior from you and your dating partner;

- learn what your potential partner wants and needs; and
- preserve your dignity—trust that things will ultimately work out well for you.

## Don't
- chase after someone to escape loneliness;
- behave in a way that disrespects your true self or causes you to feel ashamed, guilty, or foolish; or
- accept disrespectful behavior, for example, from someone who puts you down or uses "colorful" language after you've said you don't want to hear it.

Mutual respect is crucial for a good marriage. You'll be happier, ultimately, with a husband whose actions show respect for both of you. With mutual dignity, you can bring out the best in yourself and each other.

# DILIGENCE

Do you feel like giving up after a disappointing date? Or after you tried to meet somebody to date online or in person, but nothing came of it? It's easy to feel discouraged, think all the good men are taken, or fall back on another self-defeating attitude.

It's natural to lick your wounds after a disappointment. But, as they say about falling off a horse, get back on as soon as you can. You never know when or where you'll meet a future husband. So develop resilience, like the kind shown in Leah's story below.

Be thorough and persistent. When I met my husband, David, I'd already signed up for a national singles Caribbean cruise. I used to joke to friends that I'd exhausted all the possibilities at home in the San Francisco Bay Area, so I was expanding my territory. Depending on how you look at it, this quip might sound funny or desperate. But it's about diligence.

## Grieving Is Good; Then Bounce Back

Leah got engaged to Jeremy when she was thirty—a late age for a first marriage back then. She said she was thrilled when he proposed after her "long and thorough search for a husband." But Jeremy broke it off quickly, leaving her devastated. She bounced back in time to meet Brian, with whom she had much more in common. They've been married for forty-five years, with children and grandchildren.

So hang in there through the ups and downs until you find someone who's right for you—a man with whom you'll create a lasting, loving marriage. Here's to your successful journey!

# E is for

- Easy Does It
- Empathy
- Expectations (for Dating)

## EASY DOES IT

Always good advice, and especially true for dating a new person. Stay calm and relaxed. Don't wonder if he likes you. Enjoy yourself in the moment while getting to know him. If you're worried about making a good impression, you'll probably appear stiff or like you're trying too hard. It's much better to trust that if he's not "the one," someone else will be. So be your beautiful, natural self. Each date brings you closer, sooner or later, to marriage.

## EMPATHY

*Empathy is truly the heart of the relationship.*
—Carin Goldstein, MFT

Can you talk to him about your feelings, hopes, goals, and dreams? Does he listen and respond empathically? If he does, wow! If he doesn't, don't necessarily rule him out. Many men tend to jump in with a solution or a judgment when a woman just wants to be heard[1] because they are, um, men.

Emotionally available men do exist. And just about all of us, men and women, can gain more skill in empathic listening.

## Empathy Can Be Learned

If he's basically caring, he can probably learn to show more compassion. You might tell him, gently, before venting, that you would like to be heard and understood, not "fixed." When he does listen thoughtfully, tell him how much it means to you that he's really there for you. Your compliment is likely to inspire more of the same from him next time. So, do remember to keep telling him that you value him for listening.

You might wish he could read your mind, but you cannot expect him to. This is why it is so important to tell him, again gently, what you need.

You can also teach compassion by example. When you respond empathically to a man, you are a role model. The more you do this, the more likely he'll catch on and respond similarly to you.

Empathy is a trait also worth developing for relating to yourself. Many of my therapy clients first need to learn to show compassion for themselves before becoming more empathic toward a relationship partner.

## When Our Own Needs Interfere

At times, our needs and issues can block us from being receptive to another's. It can be challenging to set ourselves aside for long enough to allow space for others' self-expression.

It's helpful to give ourselves and each other some slack. Suppose someone makes a judgmental remark. The comment may hurt your feelings, but don't strike back. Instead, center yourself, perhaps by taking a few breaths; you can even close your eyes for a moment or two.

His statement may say more about him than about you. You needn't take it personally. He may well have picked up a habit of becoming critical when feeling stressed because he grew up in a family with lots of blaming. Depending on how severe his issue is, you may want to tell him that you'd like him to respond with more acceptance and see how that goes, or you may decide he's not for you.

## Sometimes It Takes a Woman

Men may be sensitive to a partner's concerns, and often a woman can help them. Yet sometimes it takes a woman to show the empathy you crave. I don't remember who hurt my feelings or about what, but I recall telling my usually empathic husband how upset I was. He said something like, "Let it go. It's no big deal." He was trying to be supportive, but I couldn't let it go.

Then I talked to a female friend. She looked at me and said, "Bummer."

My angst melted away. I felt understood.

But don't blame my husband or his gender. We may have different strengths. Vive la différence!

Do look for empathy in a potential marriage partner, but not for perfection. If your "diamond in the rough" needs a bit of improvement, he may be willing to grow in this area. If he's emotionally healthy overall, his store of empathy, deep down inside, can be mined. Sometimes it's hard to know if his seeming lack of empathy is a shortcoming that may improve over time. When you're emotionally involved, you may miss the signs of someone unlikely to change. If you're not sure, a wise friend or therapist should be able to help you gain clarity.

# EXPECTATIONS (FOR DATING)

By keeping your dating expectations realistic, you'll have more enjoyable experiences. Approach meeting and dating with an open mind. If you're tempted to judge instantly whether someone is right for you, you'll feel and appear stressed. With an accepting mindset on your part, he's more likely to see you as the vibrant, fun person you are.

Focus mainly on now. Trust that you'll be with the right man at the right time. If you take care of the moment by viewing dating as an adventure and a learning experience, the future will take care of itself.

Another topic, Expectations for Marriage, on page 193, shows the difference between realistic and unrealistic beliefs. Holding realistic ones contributes enormously to a fulfilling relationship.

# F is for

- ○ Faith
- ○ Feelings
- ○ Flexibility
- ○ Friendship
- ○ Fun

## FAITH

Many singles are conflicted about marrying. They yearn for marriage but fear it won't work out because troubled marriages and divorces have become common.

### How to Gain Faith: Katie's Story

Ten years after her divorce, Katie, a flight attendant in her late thirties, yearned to marry again. But she feared another failure. Her good friends were either divorced or had never married. Cynical about marriage, they reinforced her skepticism.

Katie was in a relationship with Stanley, a divorced pilot. Besides being anti-marriage, he wasn't emotionally supportive or reliable. He often broke dates on short notice. Katie seemed to be settling for less than what she truly wanted.

But Katie didn't give up on marrying. Here's how she gained faith in her ability to succeed. She decided to

- *learn what it takes to create a fulfilling marriage.*

  Katie started going to talks by marriage and relationship experts. She learned that spouses should go out on a weekly date together and on mini-vacations and longer ones. She read books and listened to podcasts about how to communicate positively.

- *befriend happily married people as advisors and role models.*

  Katie confided in Jackie, a married flight attendant in the crew she traveled with, about her frustrating search for a husband. Jackie told her, "It's not that Prince Charming is going to appear suddenly; it's more like you find a good man and help him become your 'prince' by how you relate to him. You can do it."

  Katie joined a hiking group that included singles and couples. She became friendly with some of the couples she met who were happy together. Katie realized that she could do better than Stanley and stopped seeing him.

- *gain self-understanding via psychotherapy.*

  Katie realized that Stanley was one in a series of men with whom she'd stayed too long in going-nowhere relationships after her divorce. Wanting to overcome her pattern, she began a course of therapy. Her therapist listened well. Katie trusted him and felt understood.

  Katie began spending time with marriage-minded men. She realized she was finding flimsy excuses to reject potential husbands. By staying single, she wouldn't have to risk being in another unhappy marriage.

## Faith Can Be Contagious

Katie's story shows how faith can be contagious. She gained trust that she could succeed in marriage by befriending happily married couples and relying on other people who bolstered her confidence.

Consequently, she became confident enough to end her last unsatisfying relationship and commit to a lifelong, fulfilling one. She's now been happily married for twenty-five years.

It takes a leap of faith to marry. By learning how to create a great marriage, developing realistic expectations, and gaining confidence in your ability to succeed, you can create a lasting, loving union.

# FEELINGS

Tune into your feelings to help assess whether a man is right for you. But keep your brain in charge of your decisions. It's easy for many of us to get carried away with feelings of infatuation, typically based on fantasy.

When the two of you are together, it's more important to feel good about both him and yourself, be comfortable being genuine when you're with him, and feel valued by him for being your unique, unpretentious self. As you get to know each other, feelings of fondness, compatibility, and comfort that emerge over time are more reliable signs of a stable future together than feelings of initial ecstasy.

So trust your feelings, for the most part, but keep your brain in charge.

# FLEXIBILITY

Flexibility is a sign of mental health, as psychiatrist Tom Smith used to say when we were colleagues at San Francisco's Alcoholism Evaluation and Treatment Center. I was single then and in my late twenties. The men I dated were usually flexible. They had to be because it was often my way or the highway about what restaurants we'd go to, things we'd do, and so on.

But I thought Tom was talking about our patients, not me! Although I was the agency's couple therapy expert, I was not yet ready for marriage. I dated a lot but was more interested in getting my way than forming a sound, lasting relationship.

## A Key Element for Good Marriage

Now that I've been married for thirty-three years, I can say that flexibility is also a key to a happy marriage. It helps to have a supportive spouse, but both partners gain happiness by living in awareness of the other's wants and needs as well as their own.

Of course, you should still have boundaries, not twist yourself into a pretzel. You don't want to fall into the trap of wanting so much to please your partner that you get confused about who you are and lose sight of your own needs.

How do we learn to practice flexibility in a way that respects both our own and our partner's needs? Here are a few ideas:

"The main thing is to keep the main thing the main thing," states Stephen Covey, author of *The Seven Habits of Highly Effective People*. Applying his advice to marriage helps change rigid patterns into more flexible ways of relating. If your main goal is to create a good marriage, then doing what it takes to do this should be more important than getting your way about every little thing.

## Flexibility Advice

Early in my marriage, a wise friend advised me, "Don't argue with your husband about anything but your child's education." She knew that for me, this was the priority where I'd need to show my backbone. For you, it could be something else. "Choose your battles" is as relevant to marriage as to child rearing. When both partners are willing to bend regarding relatively minor concerns, they are creating a good marriage. While neither is keeping score, both will appreciate how each accommodates the other. Such spouses will feel secure, safe, loved, and loving.

## How to Be Flexible in Your Relationship

Take a look at the sketches below, which show Keith Rice's tip for a good marriage. Here's how he explained how a couple could adapt to and accommodate each other:

1. Keith raised his hands in front of his chest.
2. He pressed the fingertips of one hand against the fingertips of the opposing hand and said, "Here's how it looks when each of you insists on getting your way."
3. Then, keeping all fingers spread out, he unlocked them from pushing against each other.
4. He then slowly moved his hands closer together but placed the fingers of each hand into the spaces between the fingers of the other hand. "Here's a good marriage," he said.

## Two Ways Couples Communicate.

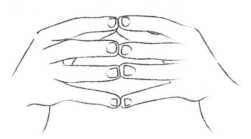

## Blocking each other.

*Making space for each other.*

Eureka! In step four, he showed how spouses make room for each other's feelings, wants, and needs. Demanding to have things go our way can work for a while, but eventually the relationship will suffer because no one wants to feel bullied by a dictator.

I learned to let go more often—to do things my husband's way when it's no big deal. But when something is important to me, I'll speak up. In a healthy relationship, partners want to please each other. They give space to each other for self-expression and for gaining what they desire or need.

## If I Can Grow, So Can You

My husband, David, is quite flexible. On a scale of one to ten, he'd get an eight or nine. When writing this entry, I asked him, "How flexible would you rate me when we first got married?"

"Three," he said.

"And now that we've been married for so long?" I wondered.

"Seven."

Good enough for now, I thought, with room to grow.

# FRIENDSHIP

*Marriages are forms of super friendship.*
—JOHN F. HELLIWELL, Senior Fellow of
the Canadian Institute for Advanced Research

Some marriages begin with love at first sight. Usually, but not always, they fail after the initial buzz wears off. Others start with a friendship that grows into love. This sort of marriage is more likely to succeed in the long run.[1]

I don't trust love at first sight: fantasy and romantic longings fuel instant infatuation. The passion is terrific. But it's not the main ingredient for an everyday fulfilling, lasting marriage. Romance is more like a condiment to spice things up.

Spice is excellent, but it's there to enhance what's already nourishing. If a marriage lacks friendship, romance and attraction will fade, or the relationship won't be satisfying overall.

## Should Your Husband Be Your BFF (Best Friend Forever)?

Ample research confirms that friendship is the main ingredient for a lasting, fulfilling relationship. When the British Household Panel Survey asked people about their closest friends, half of them said it was their spouse. For those who called their partner their best friend, the benefits of marriage were about twice as large as for those who didn't.[2] Researcher John F. Helliwell calls friendship between couples "the secret ingredient of the sauce for successful marriage." He states that it's logical to conclude that happiness in marriage "has less to do with your social status or financial stability, and more to do with sharing wedding bands with your BFF."[3]

## Friendship with a Partner Fosters Better Sex

Researchers found that valuing your friendship with your partner helps create relationships with more commitment and love, and greater sexual satisfaction.[4]

What qualities do you value in a good friend? Are you drawn to someone with similar values, who supports, respects, and understands you? A trustworthy person with whom you enjoy talking, laughing, and just hanging out?

Of course, no matter how great a man is, he cannot meet *all* of your needs; no one person can do that for another. Supportive women friends can fill the gap. Treasure yours, keep in touch, and spend quality time with them. Freeing your potential—or actual—husband from the absurd expectation to be your "everything" supports both of you and your relationship.

After marriage, yes, romance and sex should spice things up. But most of your time together will be spent relaxing, talking, eating meals, and dealing with chores and other responsibilities.

A husband who is your best friend will be there for the happy times and the challenging ones.

## Friendship with Women

Do you and your friends support each other around meeting men and dating? It can help to go with a friend to events where single men are present. Just by relaxing and being yourselves— talking, smiling, and maybe laughing together—you'll sparkle and attract men like bees to honey.

Even if you don't meet a man who interests you, you're likely to be glad you went anyway because you enjoyed being with your friend.

If you don't currently have this type of friend, you might find one at an event you go to on your own, so keep your eyes open to meet your new pal.

# FUN

A man might seem to have all the basics. He could be good-looking, caring, and share your values and some interests. But is he *fun* to be with? While it's not realistic to expect to be continually entertained or excited by him, if you often feel bored in his presence, move on.

The exception to this guideline is feeling bored or depressed because of your own life circumstances. You can't fairly expect someone else to make a life for you. Make sure to do this for yourself. Cultivate your interests and try new things. You'll be happier and more appealing.

# G is for

- Goal
- Grace
- Gratitude
- Grieving
- Grit
- Gumption

## GOAL

As any successful person in sales would say, you'll save time by qualifying your prospects.

If you want marriage, make sure to find out if the man you're interested in is looking for commitment.

Of course, it's not the first question to ask him. But before getting emotionally involved, it's crucial to find out what sort of relationship he has in mind. You may sense this from his demeanor. But if you're not sure, you can ask him casually, when the time feels right, perhaps by the third date, what he wants in life. If the word *marriage* or *family* doesn't come up, you can follow up by calmly asking whether he wants to marry. Your tone should imply that you're referring to the idea of marriage in general, not about marriage to you, because you barely know each other at this point.

His answer is your green or red light, telling you whether to keep seeing him or move on.

Sounds simple, right? But if you're spending time with a man who doesn't want to commit, ask yourself whether *you* honestly want to marry.

Many women stay in a relationship with a man who doesn't want marriage. They hope he'll change. Sometimes he does marry the woman, and it works out okay. Probably more often, he either doesn't marry her or does so under pressure and then holds a long-term grudge.

## Is Your Goal Really Marriage?

Cindy, fifty-two, is a petite, perky blond attorney who said she wanted to get past whatever was keeping her single. During her first session, Cindy said she was dating and enjoying romantic weekend getaways with a man who said he didn't want to get married.

I wondered aloud, "If you want to get married and he doesn't, why do you keep seeing him?" She nodded thoughtfully.

A couple of days later, she called to cancel her next appointment. "Thank you for helping me get clear," she said. "I've thought it over. I realize that I don't want to get married."

I think Cindy was conflicted. Part of her wanted marriage. A bigger part of her feared she'd fail at it, which is why she stayed in a casual relationship instead of looking for a serious one.

I believe that, deep down inside, everyone yearns for a soul mate. But not everyone is ready to commit to marriage. If you are clear that your goal is marriage, it's essential to learn whether the man you like is also marriage minded.

People are available to support you. Let them know you're looking for marriage. Follow up on their suggestions that resonate with you, such as offers for introductions, information about internet dating sites, events where you might meet someone, and so on.

### Getting Past What Might Be in Your Way

Some women sabotage themselves unwittingly. Do you reject a good man because he has a minor flaw? Because he doesn't conform to fairy-tale expectations? Or because you don't tell him when he does something that annoys you? That behavior could have resulted from a misunderstanding, or it might change if he knew how you felt.

So be honest with yourself and with him. Being curious and forthright should lead you to make the right decisions along your journey to success.

Dating can have ups and downs, bumps along the way. Courage and perseverance are excellent traits to foster within yourself while keeping your essential purpose in mind. There is great strength in having a goal and persevering.

# GRACE

*Grace* can mean charm, a fine quality to cultivate in ourselves. As in the song "Amazing Grace," it means unearned kindness. You may be its giver or receiver.

Being pleasant to people you meet and date, even if you feel that they don't deserve it, is good for you, them, and the planet. This doesn't mean being a pushover. Kindness means treating others with the sort of respect they deserve as human beings. We all have virtues and shortcomings. When someone's flaws seem to be screaming at you, try taking a few quiet breaths. Then accept that they're doing the best they can at the time.

Yet most of us are likely to be thrown off-balance sometimes by rude behavior.

### Jenny's Story

Harold tested Jenny's ability to respond graciously. Jenny had recently been fired from a prestigious job she'd held for five years. She was feeling lost and hopeless at a party where Harold was present. Jenny barely knew him; he was a friend of a friend. When they recognized each other, she told him that she was now unemployed, thinking he'd be supportive.

He said, "It's too bad that you don't have any skills." He then suggested that she go back to his place, presumably for sex.

*That's all he thinks I'm useful for,* Jenny thought, disgusted with him and also with herself for opening up emotionally to someone so boorish. She went home feeling awful.

## Showing Grace Is an Option

Eleanor Roosevelt said that no one can make you feel inferior without your consent. We have options; showing grace is a good one. We do not need to retreat into self-pity, as Jenny did, or to lash out vengefully. Either of these responses may feel natural, but neither is gracious to yourself or the offender.

Using Jenny as an example, here's how to switch to a gracious mode when someone treats you ungraciously: First, notice what you are feeling. Typical feelings in such situations are hurt or anger about being insulted, devalued, or manipulated. When we experience them, it's easy to feel off-balance. Jenny might start to calm herself by taking a few slow, deep breaths.

## Switching to Grace via Self-Talk

Next, she could practice the five-step self-talk communication technique described by psychologist Dr. Pamela Butler, author of *Talking to Yourself: How Cognitive Behavior Therapy Can Change Your Life.* Here's how Jenny might follow the five steps, paraphrased below, to restore herself to a more gracious state:

### Step #1. *Notice what you are feeling and thinking.*

Jenny might have been thinking, *He's a creep to treat me this way,* or *I'm worthless except as a sex object.*

Step #2. *Ask yourself: Is what I am telling myself helpful?*
Jenny answers that it is not helpful because it keeps her feeling bad about both Harold and herself.

Step #3. *Ask yourself: What is driving me to talk to myself this way?*
Jenny says her negative self-talk comes from her "judge," which labels people as bad or wrong. Jenny now tells herself, *I'm blaming both him for making me feel crummy and myself for being a mess.*

Step #4. *Give yourself better self-talk.*
Jenny tells herself, *I don't need to tolerate boorish behavior or let this person define me. When a situation feels toxic, I can politely excuse myself. I can be courteous even to someone who's not behaving decently—by not taking it personally. Uncouth behavior is about the person who acts that way. It's not about me.*

Step #5. *Form your action plan.*
Jenny decides to be more gracious when someone is insensitive. She also resolves to be more cautious about with whom she'll share her personal details. She will strive to be pleasant to all yet keep her distance from rude people. *I need to be nice to myself too*, she'll say.

## Why Respond Graciously?

Whether we're single or married, we're sometimes likely to find ourselves in situations where our buttons get pushed. Our impulse might be to retreat or strike back. Doing so creates a vicious cycle of self-defeating behavior. An angry response leads to another one or to your blaming yourself for allowing someone to mistreat you. It is much healthier for all concerned to respond to a provocation with grace.

# GRATITUDE

*There is more hunger for love and*
*appreciation in this world than for bread.*
—Mother Teresa

Psychologist John Gottman's research reveals that compliments outnumber criticisms by at least five to one in good marriages. It makes sense to apply a similar ratio in dating situations.

So notice what you value in a man you like and tell him. Your sincere compliments might make his day. They're also likely to foster a deeper connection between the two of you.

## How to Give a Compliment

Here are some examples of how to give a good compliment:

- "I appreciate you for your thoughtfulness in suggesting that we eat at the restaurant you know is my favorite."
- "I like how you look in that blue shirt. It brings out the blue color of your eyes."
- "Thank you for cooking dinner. I love how you made the pasta with pesto, mushrooms, and olives."
- "I appreciate you for talking with me about my work situation. I liked how you listened, asked questions, and helped me figure out what to do next."
- "I'm impressed with how conscientious you were in completing that detailed report for work on Tuesday night."

These ways of expressing appreciation have two things in common. First, they all feature I-statements, meaning they are personal expressions that come from the heart. They do not sound like objective evaluations, like "You were thoughtful," "You're a good cook," or "You're a good listener." Next, they are specific; that is, they mention details. She says exactly what she liked about his cooking, even going so far as to note the ingredients. She says that the shirt was *blue* and brought out the blue color of his eyes.

## Enhancing Your Appreciation

Here are ways to enhance your compliments:

- Use open body language and a warm vocal tone. Smile and make soft eye contact.
- Compliment positive character traits: "I appreciated your *consideration* in calling to let me know you'd be late."
- Remember to be specific.

## Responding to a Compliment

When he compliments you, listen silently, then thank him. If you don't think you deserve the compliment, accept it anyway. Disagreeing with his praise is like throwing the gift in his face. If he says how great you look in your new dress and you say, "I look fat," you're saying, "I don't want your compliment. You made a mistake." If you haven't learned to accept a compliment, practice. Smile graciously and say, "Thank you!" This is important.

## Showing Gratitude Has Countless Benefits

Expressing gratitude reinforces behaviors you like. If you tell him that you think he looks great in his leather jacket, he'll probably wear it more often. If you praise his lasagna, he'll probably want to cook it for you again.

Noticing excellent traits in someone produces a ripple effect. You then focus more often on what you like about him and other people too. So expressing gratitude adds to your reservoir of optimism and sense of well-being. You'll keep the warm feelings flowing by paying good attention to what's going well and communicating your appreciation often.

# GRIEVING

Do you have unfinished business? Many of us do. It's important to gain closure about a past relationship before expecting to succeed in a new one.

In the psychological sense, closure means gaining an emotional conclusion to a difficult life situation, such as losing a romantic partner, spouse, or parent. Grieving produces closure. Some people need to grieve over what was lacking if they grew up in an unhealthy family or home environment.

## Loss of a Romantic Partner

Are you still emotionally attached to someone who's no longer in your life? Some people try to quickly replace a former partner they thought was *the one* before grieving the loss. They may crave reassurance of their desirability, companionship, or something else. But they are still quite vulnerable because they haven't yet cleared the decks. So their new relationship is not likely to be satisfying over time.

What if you still love him and can't believe it's over? Maybe you thought the relationship was serious, but he didn't.

If you rush into a new relationship before processing your thoughts and feelings about a previous one, you can come across as needy, tense, or controlling. Or you may choose someone who's not right for you. By first taking care of your unfinished business, you'll be more confident, relaxed, and self-accepting.

## Julie's Pattern

Julie hoped to marry. A successful executive with an engaging personality, she attracted men easily—when she was ready. *Ready* is the crucial word. After each going-nowhere relationship ended, her self-esteem plummeted. She would be miserable for a long time and not ready for a new relationship. Finally, she would return to her vibrant, confident state and attract a new man. When that relationship fell apart, so would she, and the cycle continued.

## Grieving Ultimately Boosts Happiness

Happy people attract happy people. By accepting all of our feelings around a loss, we clear out our insides. A sense of contentment returns.

Grieving a failed relationship can include learning from the past. Think "no mistakes, only lessons." Julie recognized her pattern: She became sexually and emotionally involved with men who wanted a no-strings-attached, casual dating relationship. And she rejected men who were ready for marriage.

A wise friend told Julie, "If you don't know the difference between sex and love, don't have sex." With the support of her therapist, Julie stayed on course toward her goal of marrying. She learned to determine whether a man was ready for a serious relationship before letting herself become attached emotionally.

As Julie became more confident about her ability to succeed in marriage, she met and dated men who shared her goal. She was attracted to Will and enjoyed their growing friendship. Julie's nonverbal message was that she liked him very much, and she was not available for sex without commitment.

Julie and Will have been happily married for over twenty years and enjoy great sex.

## Grieving the Loss of a Spouse

After losing her husband through divorce or death, a woman is likely to feel devastated and overwhelmed. From moment to moment, she may feel angry, hurt, shocked, betrayed, numb, guilty, abandoned, or empty. She has lost her lover, companion, and a big piece of her identity because she is no longer a wife.

The effects of such a loss are typically long-lasting. There is no timetable for grieving. But the sooner you allow yourself to experience your uncensored thoughts and emotions and express them to a caring friend, skilled therapist, grief counselor, or another empathic listener, the sooner you can start to recover.

Again, there is no timetable. If you're still filled with complicated emotions after a death or divorce, an attempt to succeed in
a new relationship is likely to be premature. When you're ready
to move on, you will.

## Unprocessed Feelings after Divorce Cause Problems

Year after year, Amanda attends an annual singles weekend
retreat where I'm a speaker. She's pretty, smart, and charming.
I overheard her tell a man, while her teenage daughter stood
nearby, about what a louse her ex-husband is.

How can Amanda be fully present with a new man when she's
so full of resentment toward her ex that she unloads it on a virtual
stranger? My heart went out to both her and her daughter. When
a mother airs her complaints about her daughter's father in her
daughter's presence, she drives a wedge between the two of them.

Also, bad-mouthing your ex may repel someone who could
be right for you and attract someone who is not suitable for you.

Before she is ready for a good relationship, Amanda will
need to find healthier ways to grieve and take responsibility for
any part she may have played in her marriage's failure.

## Grieving the Loss of a Parent

Women who lost a father, stepfather, or another father figure
during their childhood, whether through a divorce, abandonment, or death, will probably need to grieve before they can
create a successful marriage.

To a child, divorce is a massive betrayal of trust. Children believe
that their parents will stay together and always be there for them.
Grieving is a clearing process. It makes it possible for our minds
and hearts to be fully present for a current or future relationship.

## How to Grieve

People find many ways to grieve. Journaling or talking with sensitive friends about your thoughts, feelings, and memories can

be helpful. So can allowing yourself to release pent-up emotions by crying for as long as you need to. Many people gain help via therapy, grief counseling, or a grief support group. By doing whatever it takes to process a loss, we make room for something great to enter.

*She's washing that man
right out of her hair.*

# GRIT

Some marriage-minded women find their match quickly. For others, the process is more like a marathon than a sprint.

What does it take to finish a marathon? It takes grit.

Angela Duckworth, PhD, author of *Grit: The Power of Passion and Perseverance*, provides convincing evidence that what drives success is a unique combination of passion and long-term perseverance.

In general, we succeed by setting a goal about which we feel passionate, then doing what it takes for as long as it takes to achieve that goal. We keep moving forward and overcome obstacles along the way.

What does a long-distance runner do? She doesn't sprint because she'll tire out too soon. She first prepares herself by learning how to succeed. She cultivates the ability to bounce back when disappointed by setbacks. She relaxes and keeps moving forward until she reaches her destination.

So hang in there. Stay on track in your journey toward marriage.

# GUMPTION

*Gumption* is defined as "the ability to decide what is best to do in a particular situation and to do it with energy and determination."[1]

I showed gumption at a singles event at a social hall. My friend Sally and another woman she knew met men they liked. They wanted to continue the evening at a nearby bar, and Sally was my ride home. So I reluctantly agreed to go with her, adding that I didn't want to be a fifth wheel. She suggested that I invite others to join us.

As our paths crossed near the dessert table, I asked a pleasant-looking man if he wanted to go. Then I asked another. Both said yes. I'm not much of a bar person, but I mustered up the gumption to invite two strangers to come along.

If you think you need to wait for him to start a conversation, you might avoid meeting a wonderful man. Many shy guys are delighted when a woman makes the first move. So show gumption. A simple "hello" is fine. Also, a smile.

The first man I invited to join us at the bar proposed to me eight months later. I said yes.

# H is for

- O Happy
- O Healing
- O Honesty
- O Hookups
- O Humility
- O Humor

## HAPPY

*Folks are usually about as happy as
they make their minds up to be.*
—ABRAHAM LINCOLN

Create your happiness while single or married. Do not expect
a potential or actual husband to do it for you. Happiness is an
inside job. So don't postpone it.

Ask yourself, "What small thing can I do today that brings
me pleasure?" Then do it.

## HEALING

I'm glad I had good therapy by the time I met the man I married.
I needed to understand how my parents' divorce had influenced

my relationship pattern. Eventually, I healed enough to allow marriage-minded men into my life and to recognize the difference between them and the other sort.

Many people resist gaining self-understanding. They may be afraid of reviving a painful memory or discovering a truth about themselves that feels uncomfortable. They may subconsciously believe that they can't succeed in marriage.

## The Consequence of Not Healing

Megan is a beautiful brunette in her sixties. Men are drawn to her slim figure, lush hair, and peaches-and-cream complexion. Once they meet her, they also value her razor-sharp wit. She's sweet, compassionate, and sensitive. Several of her confidants say Megan is their best friend.

Megan says she's always wanted to marry. Yet she continues to become involved with men who want a casual, hookup-style relationship. She doesn't believe she deserves more.

Megan grew up with a father who devalued her because of her scoliosis, a curvature of the spine, which is invisible to most people. She says he treated her "like I was incompetent and bound to fail at anything I tried to do."

Meanwhile, she heard her father frequently praise her younger brother for being smart and capable, which were excellent qualities for the son he was grooming to head his chain of furniture stores eventually.

## Therapy Can Help

How parents treat us when we're young can affect our self-esteem as adults. Megan's father's criticism continues to hold her back from appreciating her many terrific traits. Her mother was supportive but unable to outweigh her father's influence.

Megan tried therapy for a short time but didn't stick with it. She said she liked her therapist, but she didn't believe therapy would help her.

If something from your past might be blocking you from moving toward marriage, and you haven't been able to progress on your own, I cannot overstate the value of receiving good therapy and staying with it to help you heal. (See Therapy, page 167.)

# HONESTY

Honesty is a vital trait to look for in a partner. Be honest with him—and with yourself. Being honest with a relationship partner is not just about telling the truth. It's about saying it in a way that is respectful and helpful. Honesty is not blurting out anything on your mind with no regard for the other person's feelings. When that happens, the wounded feelings that result are more likely to create distance between the two of you than bring about a change you want in the other person.

## Being Honest with Him

Suppose you don't like hearing him complain excessively about a boss or a former relationship partner. As he goes on and on, you run out of patience. Your chest tightens, or you forget to breathe. You might feel tempted to tell him he's ridiculous, unreasonable, or sick in the head. Or you might say nothing and stop responding to his texts or calls.

If instead, you decide to be honest *and* caring, you might say something calmly like, "I understand this has been frustrating for you. But I'm starting to feel a bit overwhelmed. Can we talk about something else for a while?"

## Being Honest with Yourself

The hardest person to be honest with is often yourself. Many marriage-minded women stay too long in a going-nowhere relationship because they don't accept the truth that the man is not likely to change. Or they see a bad character trait that should be a deal breaker. Yet they remain involved with the person, denying that a problem exists. They ignore, minimize, or make excuses, hoping things will improve.

When you long for things to work out well, it's vital to gain objectivity about whether you can create a satisfying marriage with someone. To gain insight into whether you might be fooling yourself, you can talk with a wise friend, therapist, or professional counselor.

## Detecting Dishonesty

The simple way to find out if a man is honest with you or with himself is to notice whether his actions are consistent with his words. For example, he may say he doesn't believe in gossiping but then tell you sordid details about an acquaintance that are none of your business. His inconsistency tells you that he's not honest with himself or you. You also know now not to trust him with your private matters.

When it comes to finding out whether a man is marriage minded—which I recommend doing reasonably early in a relationship—how do you know if he's answering honestly? You might find out by reading between the lines of what he says or by following up on his answer with another question.

When one of my clients asked a man she was dating if he was interested in marrying—in general, not referring to herself—he responded, "I'm not opposed to marriage." I took that to mean he was hedging his bets. He wanted to keep dating her, but if he sincerely hoped to marry in the relatively near future, he would have answered more directly with a simple "yes" or a nod of the head.

You might want to begin this conversation by asking what he wants out of life or how he views his future. If he doesn't mention marriage, you can gently ask him whether he hopes to marry.

If a man is pressing for sex in an uncommitted relationship, that can be an excellent time to determine his intentions. As Ellie did with Henry (page 155), you might say, "Do you mind if I ask you a personal question? Are you interested in marrying?" If he says yes, how do you know if he's telling the truth or saying what he thinks you want to hear? If it's the latter, you might surprise him by asking, "When?" If he hesitates, as Henry did, he's not telling the truth.

By making honesty a way of life and seeking a spouse who does the same, you're on your way to a relationship with mutual trust.

# HOOKUPS

Although hooking up is probably talked about more openly now, it's nothing new.

Whether it's a "friends with benefits" situation or two virtual strangers deciding to have no-strings-attached sex, many people say they enjoy the physical part and can stay emotionally detached.

However, a problem arises when one hookup partner, usually the woman, is more interested than the other in a serious relationship. Sometimes the man and woman do end up marrying. However, research finds that such unions are the least likely to be successful.

"We found that people who said their relationship began by hooking up reported lower marital quality than people who didn't start their relationship by hooking up," states Galena Rhoades, a research associate professor of psychology at the University of Denver. She is co-author of the report from the National Marriage Project at the University of Virginia in Charlottesville.[1]

In general, hooking up is not a good idea for women who want marriage. So if you want a husband and feel lonely in bed, grab your teddy bear.

# HUMILITY

*Who is wise? He who learns from every person.*
—Pirkei Avot[2]

Humility means accepting the truth that you are not always right and that others have something to offer. It's the opposite of coming across as boastful or self-important.

Humility is an essential trait for constructive dating and marriage. You show humility by

- letting go of thinking you need to appear perfect;
- acknowledging, at least to yourself, both your shortcomings and strengths;
- making space for others to express themselves while you listen attentively; and
- being curious, not judgmental, when someone's opinions or politics differ from yours.

## Humility Means Accepting Differences

Typically couples who see me for therapy start out thinking their partner is wrong for being different. One spouse might have an authoritarian style of raising children; the other is more permissive. One might be more liberal and the other more conservative. Early bird, night owl. Vegetarian, carnivore, and so on.

Relationships thrive when we can accept differences. It can be challenging to let go of thinking that our way is better. Yet when opposing views occur, usually neither one is right nor wrong. We're just different, and that can be okay.

## Humility Is a Strength

Some people confuse humility with weakness. But it requires a type of inner power to accept that we don't have all the answers, to refrain from injecting our point of view before really hearing what the other person has to say.

A willingness to learn from others takes strength. It means that when tempted to act like a rigid oak tree, you become more like a willow that bends with the wind. It means that while recognizing your worth, you can set yourself aside enough to learn about someone you're getting to know. So listen with interest when he shares his thoughts, feelings, hopes, and dreams.

## Subduing the Urge to Fight or Flee

It can be hard to stay humble when treated disrespectfully. If provoked, you may want to lash out, freeze, shut down, or run away. Instead of entering a fight-or-flight mode, you'll show strength by setting aside your ego and responding thoughtfully.

Depending on the situation, you may first want to take a few deep breaths to center yourself. The person's rudeness probably reflects his insecurity. So don't take it personally if he belittles you. You may choose to tell him, in a mild voice, how you'd prefer him to behave toward you. No matter how he responds, you'll have cleared the air, whether or not you decide to continue seeing him.

## Showing Humility on a Date

You show humility by being a good listener and by knowing you don't have all the answers. When Lena met Weston, she had just started her own business and told him she didn't know if it would succeed. They've been married for fifteen years. He still remembers that he liked her for "not putting on airs."

# HUMOR

It's heartwarming when the two of you laugh together about situations and yourselves—respectfully, of course. Is "sense of humor" on your list of traits you want in a spouse?

# I is for

- ○ I-Statements
- ○ Independent
- ○ Interdependent
- ○ Interesting

## I-STATEMENTS

How do you talk to someone about a sensitive topic? If he says something that makes you uneasy, do you feel tightness in your throat, chest, or elsewhere? Forget to breathe?

Maybe you either change the subject or withdraw. If you're feeling combative, you might tell the person that he's selfish, unreasonable, or inconsiderate.

*Reacting* means doing or saying the first thing that pops into your mind. If you routinely do whatever someone asks you to do when you'd prefer not to do it, you'll probably become resentful. If instead of giving in, you belittle or ignore the person, he'll get upset.

By responding to a provocation thoughtfully, using I-statements instead of acting impulsively, you can create friendlier communications.

## What's an I-Statement?

I-statements are an essential communication skill. They usually begin with the word *I*. I-statements provide a simple, powerful way to state our thoughts, feelings, wishes, or needs.

Examples: "*I* felt hurt when you forgot it was my birthday." "*I'd* like you to phone me if you're going to be late." I-statements tend to foster connection, cooperation, and respect.

---

### EXAMPLES OF I-STATEMENTS[1]

I appreciate _____;

I like _____;

I want; I'd rather not _____;

I feel (happy, hurt, anxious, resentful, grateful, sad, etc.) when you _____

(action word or phrase)

because _____.

(effect the action or event had on you)

What I would like instead is

_____.

* A good I-statement is free from expectations. It is a clear statement of how it is from your side and how you would like it to be.

---

## You-Statements

On the other hand, a you-statement typically creates distance in a relationship. It often starts with the word *you*. It usually implies that the other person is bad or wrong. Examples: "*You're* a slob. *You* always leave crumbs on the counter."

Some people think they are making an I-statement, but it's a disguised you-statement. Example: "I feel that *you are a slob* when you leave crumbs on the kitchen counter." The sentence starts with *I*, but it's expressing a negative judgment.

This comment could be changed into a true I-statement instead by saying, "I feel annoyed when you leave crumbs on the counter." You can then say what you would like to occur, using an I-statement: "I'd appreciate it if you would clean the counter after making your sandwich."

## What an I-Statement Communicates

An I-statement is a clear message that can express

- what you are thinking, e.g., "I think it's important to keep agreements;"
- how you are feeling, e.g., "I like it when you open the car door for me;"
- why you feel the way you do, e.g., "because when you open a door for me, I feel appreciated as a woman;"
- what you want or need, e.g., "I want to get married;" or
- what you are prepared to do if you don't get what you want or need, e.g., "If you're not interested in a serious relationship, I'm ready to say goodbye and move on."

## Benefits of I-Statements

I-statements are powerful in dating, marriage, and elsewhere because they are likely to

- let the other person know how you feel and what you want;
- avoid arguments and misunderstandings;
- help you state your thoughts and feelings calmly;
- increase clarity and understanding; and
- foster a heartfelt connection between the two of you.

## How to Make an I-Statement

By following these steps for making an I-statement, you'll be more likely to be understood and gain cooperation:

1. Say how you feel about the behavior.
2. Name the specific behavior.
3. Say what you'd like or wouldn't like to happen next time.
4. (Optional) Say what you're prepared to do if the behavior continues.

### Example:

A woman might say to a man she's been dating, "I felt uncomfortable when you flirted with the waitress last night. When you're with me, I want to feel like I'm the only woman on your mind." Now, or in the future, if the flirting happens again, she might add, "If this continues, I'm afraid I won't want to keep seeing you."

If you decide to say what you will do if your partner's behavior does not change, it's best to encourage cooperation by speaking in a friendly tone and not sounding like you're making a threat or accusation.

## Strive for Progress, Not Perfection

Assuming that you are a nice person but not a saint, you may slip at times and impulsively say something you regret. When this happens, recognize your mistake and do the repair work promptly. Be generous with your I-statements. Let your partner know that you regret what you said in a way that fits for you, such as, "I'm sorry. I wish I could erase what I said. I want to do better next time." Or, "Let me rephrase that."

## Do You Find It Hard to Make I-Statements?

If you experience serious challenges that hold you back from making I-statements or empathizing with yourself and others, therapy can help. Most of us can learn to communicate positively, even when our buttons get pushed. If making I-statements feels uncomfortable, make them anyway. Practice makes perfect. By using I-statements more often, we're likely to relate more authentically and thoughtfully to ourselves and others.

## When I-Statements Backfire

Usually, using I-statements will help you feel heard, valued, and understood. Exceptions happen, however. Some people aren't comfortable being on the receiving end of an I-statement. As children, they may have heard that it's selfish to ask directly for what you want. A parent might have let them know that it's also wrong to express angry, upset, hurt, or sad feelings.

People raised to suppress their feelings are likely to be afraid of vulnerability, which happens when we open up to share our emotions and desires. As an adult, such a person may lack self-understanding and empathy. Upon hearing your I-statements, he might feel backed into a corner and respond insensitively.

If this describes someone you like, you'll do well to show compassion. Your challenge is to state your feelings and wishes while being sensitive to the person's comfort level. You can keep the conversation light by using a warm voice, smiling, and staying relaxed.

# INDEPENDENT

If you've been doing fine on your own for some time, you may fear that marriage will cost you your freedom. The truth is that a good marriage supports you to be free because the spouses want each other's needs met.

Happy couples balance time together and apart in ways that suit both partners. They collaborate to make big decisions about things like expenses, parenting, leisure time activities, and so on. By caring to hear each other's thoughts, they bond securely over time. They create a lasting, fulfilling marriage.

## A Good Marriage Enhances Freedom

Not everyone views marriage as freedom enhancing. Randall, single and in his late forties, sees marriage as "the old ball and chain." He feels sorry for his well-paid coworker, "whose wife won't let him buy a bowling ball." Randall thought he dodged a bullet by staying single.

Dina, also in her forties, also thinks marriage would cramp her style. "I don't want to have to eat every single meal with the same person," she said.

I wondered why she thought she'd need to. My husband and I usually eat dinner together, and occasionally another meal, because we both want to. I don't know any couples who feel obliged to share three meals a day.

A "ball and chain" union forces a spouse to squeeze into a mold formed by the other. On the other hand, a good marriage fosters self-expression and growth. Spouses feel encouraged to be their true selves. They deal with issues respectfully, so each partner gets heard. They generally don't need to justify a relatively minor, affordable purchase, like a bowling ball. They give each other space to do things on their own, whether concerning meals, snacks, hobbies, or something else.

## Gaining Independence before Marrying

Elyse, an attractive woman in her fifties, came to one of my Marry with Confidence workshops. She had a floundering business as a massage therapist and was sick of her hand-to-mouth lifestyle. Elyse said that the main quality she wanted in a husband was the ability to support her financially. "Why not?" she asked. "Prostitutes get paid for sex." For her, it seemed, marriage was a socially sanctioned sex-for-money arrangement.

Poverty can wear down a person and make her feel desperate to latch onto any port in a storm. But marrying mainly for financial security is less likely to result in a lasting, satisfying union than choosing a life partner with whom you fit well emotionally, intellectually, and spiritually.

We are not living in Jane Austen's time when the sole career option for a typical middle-class woman was to find a husband who could support her comfortably. Yet Austen's heroines, who ended up with financially well-off husbands (note that this is fiction), still cared more about a man's character than his money.

Today, job and career opportunities for women are plentiful. I think most men would rather marry a woman who's financially stable than one who is barely getting by.

Also, we gain confidence and become more appealing by showing independence in other ways. Instead of waiting for a man to whisk you off to exciting activities, are you initiating them for yourself? Do you like sushi? Take yourself to a restaurant and enjoy it, alone or with a friend. By pursuing your interests, whatever they are, you'll become more happy, engaging, and vibrant.

# INTERDEPENDENT

*No man is an island.*
—JOHN DONNE[2]

After marriage, we should keep our sense of independence while knowing that no one is entirely self-sufficient. We depend on car mechanics, airplane pilots, farmers, friends, accountants, therapists, and others. We also rely on our marriage partner.

Spouses in a good marriage respect each other's individuality. Doing so enhances their relationship as romantic partners and teammates.

When I was single, I feared that marriage could cause me to lose my identity. My married friend Amy set me straight. "I think of my marriage as a three-stranded braid," she said. "One strand is me, a separate person. Another is Michael. The third strand is our relationship." I took this to mean that marriage can be a union of individuals who are both independent and interdependent.

Until recently, the roles of men and women were fixed and interdependent. Usually, the husband earned money (or brought home the kill). His wife cooked and kept the home fires burning. Today, in many successful marriages, spouses are interdependent in different ways. Either partner can be a "provider" or a homemaker. Often both jobs are shared.

If your relationship is becoming serious, think about how you'd like the two of you to be a team in marriage. Say what's important to each of you. Here are a few examples: How will you deal with money? Household responsibilities, such as cooking, shopping, cleaning, laundry, and gardening? Childcare? Diaper changing? Except for who bears children, almost everything is negotiable.

The more you think through in advance what you will rely on each other for, the more realistic your expectations will be after marriage. You and your future spouse can customize your interdependence in ways that honor each other's needs and preferences.

# INTERESTING

Some women complain that the men they meet aren't "interesting." Such comments jolt me. Interesting may be fine, but not if you expect all stimulation to come from outside yourself. Women who are already enjoying life rather than waiting for someone to light up their world attract men naturally. Doing interesting things makes us attractive to others.

You create excitement by continuing to learn and grow. By pursuing your interests, whether through work, hobbies, clubs, or something else, you feel glad to be alive. Your glow attracts like-minded people, some of whom you'll probably find interesting.

### Do You Have Enough Similar Interests?

Couples in good marriages tend to have enough similar interests to be compatible. Common interests often bring people together and then nourish the relationship. You may meet your future husband in a class or a club, on a ski slope, at a lecture, or anywhere else.

It's fine to want to marry someone you find interesting. But don't expect a husband to save you from boredom. That's a do-it-yourself job. *Interesting* is an overrated trait to look for in someone outside of yourself. If you're easily bored, I'll be blunt: Stop being boring. Find things to do that make you happy, and do them!

Suppose you're usually quite stimulated by your own life and activities. In that case, you might be happier with a sweet, calm, easygoing man than with an "interesting" one who has an unusual lifestyle, impressive accomplishments, a fascinating hobby, or something else. Do you want to be entertained, or would you feel more fulfilled by an empathic, laid-back person with whom you enjoy spending time and conversing?

## Is There Room for Both of You?

It's okay if a man is interesting, but also think about how he treats you. Ask yourself, "Does he show interest in me? Is there room for both of us in our conversations?" If your answer is yes to both questions, good! You want someone who is interested in you, not just full of himself, right?

If you are looking for a good marriage partner, chemistry should be there, of course. It's also vital for him to have the character traits that matter and for the two of you to have similar values, enough shared interests, and intellectual compatibility.

By allowing passionate feelings to take over before you know him very well, you may think of him as a perfect fairy-tale prince who's here to rescue your inner Cinderella. You're likely to be happier in the long run if you keep your brain in charge so that you'll view him realistically as a person with his unique mix of strengths and shortcomings.

## Brittany's Story

Brittany's experience shows why it's essential to maintain your individuality while in a relationship. Brittany enjoyed a successful career as a psychologist who helped many people. She wanted to marry, but something was amiss in her dating pattern. Her effervescence attracted men. She was full of life and kept busy with her varied interests and friendships—until she was in a relationship. Then, she would drop her interests and spend less time with friends.

Brittany would become so dependent on a man to make her life meaningful that she became a shell of her former self, and therefore less appealing. After each relationship ended, she would feel empty and depressed. It would take her some time to return to her happy self, who would attract a new man, then repeat the cycle.

The moral is, of course, to stay interesting. Do not lose yourself in a relationship. Stay in touch with who you are and what gives you joy. Ultimately, you'll be happier in life and marriage by striving to fulfill your potential and use your unique gifts, which you can offer to your relationship and the world. A good marriage provides a foundation that supports both partners in ways that help them keep growing as a couple and as separate individuals.

Just in case you're still wondering how to meet someone interesting, take a look in the mirror. That person just might be you!

# J is for

○ Journey
○ Joy

## JOURNEY

Do you view marriage as a destination or a journey? If you see it as a journey, you're more likely to succeed.

If you think of marriage as a destination, an end in itself, you'll probably be disappointed. When the glow fades, you'll wonder, *How could I have married this person who is so annoying?* That thought tends to surface in any marriage. Does this surprise you?

If we view marriage as a journey, we'll learn over and over how to deal well with relationship challenges as they arise. We'll see them as opportunities for growth.

Understanding that marriage is a journey means knowing that it takes ongoing energy to keep the relationship thriving. One helpful way to do this is to hold a weekly marriage meeting. (See Marriage Meetings, page 88.)[1]

Approached this way, and with an ongoing quest for self-understanding, marriage is the ultimate growth experience. By thinking and acting in ways that bring out the best in yourselves and each other, you'll create a relationship that stays fulfilling.

## Thriving in an Ever-Changing Reality

By living this way, we empathize with and support each other. We develop more sensitivity to our partner's wants and needs and our own. We can become "other-centered" without losing ourselves.

To succeed in marriage, we need to commit to an ever-changing reality as our lives and relationships evolve.

Wisely choosing your partner is the first step toward creating a fulfilling, lasting marriage. By treating marriage as a journey, we allow the glow to keep returning. We fall in love with our partner again and again.

# JOY

Whether you have a partner or hope to, do something every day that makes you happy. You'll be nurturing yourself, recharging your battery, and lighting up yourself and the world.

Like attracts like, so the energy you gain by enjoying yourself will attract emotionally healthy men. But if you're feeling down or morbidly self-absorbed, you're more likely to interest an unhappy person who might feed off your low self-esteem as a way to feel better about himself.

What if you're experiencing depression or some other mental health concern? By seeing a therapist who's a good fit for you, you're likely to recover your sense of well-being and experience more joy.

Helping others with a true spirit of selflessness can uplift you. You can gain joyful feelings by lending an ear to a coworker, friend, or family member, or by volunteering at a community organization or event. You'll feel that you matter because you have something valuable to contribute to the world. Voilà! Your self-esteem rises, and you stand straighter. You meet others with a smile because you know that we're all connected.

Many other pursuits can bring you joy. Here's a way to gain ideas for some: Think back to your childhood. Ask yourself what activities you used to enjoy. Include things you liked to do as a child, teenager, and beyond. Some of the experiences that used to delight you may still do so.

If you want more ideas for creating good times, try this exercise: Make a chart like the sample below, into which you will insert ten activities you think you'd enjoy. Fill in the blanks to state how long it's been since you've done each one, whether you do it alone or with another person (A or P), and whether or not it's free. Then state when you'll schedule each activity or what step you can take to make it happen. Here's how a partially completed chart might look:

## PLANNING SELF-NURTURING ACTIVITIES[2]

| ACTIVITY | WHEN LAST DONE | A or P | FREE OR $ | ACTION STEP/ SCHEDULE |
|---|---|---|---|---|
| Take a relaxing bath (bubbles optional) | A month ago | A | Free | Tomorrow morning |
| Go kayaking | Last summer | A or P | $ | |
| Roller-skate in a rink | A year ago | A or P | $ | The adult session this Tuesday |
| See a play | Three months ago | A or P | $ | Call friend tonight; make reservations. |
| Go to a beach | Two months ago | A or P | Free | |
| Read a novel | A few weeks ago | A | Free | |
| Go to a library | A few months ago | A | Free | Go this Friday. |
| Hike in woods | Four months ago | A or P | Free | A week from Sunday |

Using the above chart as a guide, list ten activities that you enjoy, when you last did each one, whether you can do it alone or it requires another person, and whether it's free or costs money.

Then identify when you would like to schedule each activity or what step you can take to make it happen.

In *The Artist's Way*, Julia Cameron recommends that all of us, not just artists, schedule a weekly "artist date" by devoting a block of time, at least two hours and at least once a week, to being *alone* while engaging in a self-nurturing activity. The uncensored thoughts that emerge during these times can become a springboard for new ways to address challenges we may face regarding just about anything. By doing so, we tap into our essential selves and unleash creativity. Free of the usual distractions, our minds get to wander wherever. If you're rusty in the fun department, you can find many ideas on the internet by searching for "lists of pleasurable activities" and then choosing some to do.

The idea is to be a happy, joyful person. Wouldn't you rather feel that way than needy or depleted? You have so many options for enjoyment. So why wait for someone else to make you happy? Instead, treat yourself to good times now.

When I was single, there were times I thought I couldn't be happy unless I was in a relationship. Eventually, I got over that. Once I became more content, I attracted caring, emotionally stable men. I became so good at enjoying myself solo that when one new man asked me for a Saturday night date, I suggested Sunday because I liked watching a weekly Saturday night television show.

I thought Tupperware parties were fun around that time, so I decided to host a coed one for singles. I asked some of the men I'd invited to bring a male friend, and one brought Bob, an attractive attorney. I vaguely remembered Bob, who asked me out for dinner a week later. Having fun and getting all those people together must have made me glow like a light bulb.

By filling your life with whatever makes you happy, you're likely to attract good men.

# K is for

- ○ Kindness
- ○ Knowing Yourself

## KINDNESS

*The highest form of wisdom is kindness.*
—THE TALMUD

Kindness seems like an obvious trait, not only to seek in a husband but also to instill in ourselves. Yet many women who list qualities they want in a life partner don't include kindness.

Kindness is the foundation of most major religions and enduring philosophies. A "what's in it for me" mentality, the opposite of a kindness mindset, can show up in people we meet.

### Kindness Is Key for a Good Relationship

Compassion is an essential building block of a good marriage. Partners in successful relationships live in awareness of each other's wants and needs and are mutually helpful.

When I was single, I had a sweet dog. None of my friends wanted to take care of her while I went out of town, so she boarded in a kennel. It meant a lot to me when a man I'd recently started dating offered to take care of her at his place while I was away for a few days. He took her again for a week shortly before we became engaged—even though I was going on a singles cruise! I'd signed up for that before our relationship developed. He didn't feel taken advantage of. He was simply kind; this trait, more than any other, probably endeared him to me enough to marry him.

## Making Kindness a Habit

When we do something thoughtful for someone, such as giving a gift, listening empathically, visiting a sick person, or serving a meal—solely out of goodwill, with no expectation to receive anything in return—we are likely to feel good about ourselves and the other person. You can improve two people with one simple act of kindness. It can be as simple as buying someone a cup of coffee. Doing so makes you a better person, and your thoughtfulness leaves the recipient feeling cared for and, consequently, warmer to others.

How about making it a habit to do or say at least one nice thing during each date or each time you meet a new man?

If you're finding it hard to be pleasant to someone, know that the trait that annoys us in another person may be one that we also have. Being kind is about seeing the good in ourselves and others. We all have strengths and weaknesses. Once we can view ourselves compassionately, we're naturally inclined to see others similarly.

So be kind to yourself in thought and deed. By doing so, you'll keep your cup of goodwill full enough to share much of it with others. Try it—you'll see!

# KNOWING YOURSELF

*Until you make peace with who you are,*
*you'll never be content with what you have.*
—Doris Mortman

"Who am I?" is something we can ask and answer throughout our lives because the answer keeps changing. While the essential self stays the same, our interests, values, and lifestyle can change over time.

Concerning marriage, self-knowledge means recognizing what you can contribute to a relationship and what traits you want or need in a marriage partner. (See Lists, page 79.) It can also mean identifying what internal obstacles might be preventing you from committing to marriage, although you yearn for it.

## Some of Us Are Conflicted

For a long time, while single, I thought I wanted marriage but was conflicted. Unconsciously, I feared being abandoned, which happened to both my mother and her mother. My immigrant grandmother, who spoke little English, was deserted by her husband, who left her pregnant and penniless with a four-year-old daughter, my mother's older sister. Soon after my mother was born, my grandmother was placed in a state mental hospital, where she spent the rest of her life. My mother and aunt grew up in an orphanage.

My mother agreed to divorce my father, but it was his idea. He'd pressured her for a long time. She was heartbroken. She, my sister, and I felt abandoned. When he promptly remarried and had a child a year later, we were inconsolable.

Before I'd be able to date with commitment as my real goal, I needed to trust that I could succeed in marriage. Psychotherapy helped me know myself. I recognized and moved past my pattern of staying in going-nowhere relationships and rejecting marriage-minded men.

Years earlier, a good friend told me I was ambivalent about marrying. Back then, I was gaining recognition as a skilled couples and family therapist. Her perceptive comment went in one ear and out the other. I thought the men I got involved with were commitment-phobic, not me!

Who doesn't have room to grow? I can vouch personally for the difficulty in owning things about ourselves that we're not proud of. But accepting our imperfections ultimately makes us feel more confident and whole. Consequently, we become more compassionate and accepting toward ourselves and others.

# L is for

- ○ **Lists**
- ○ **Love**
- ○ **Love Yourself**

## LISTS

Many women who hope to marry lack clarity about what traits they require in a spouse. So they may stay too long with someone who's not right for them. Some women settle for less than they deserve in a partner because they don't recognize their own excellent traits. They might reject someone because of an imperfection, although that person might have all the features they need in a husband.

I ask women in my Marry with Confidence workshops to make three lists. By creating each list thoughtfully, you're likely to

- gain clarity about the qualities you value in a spouse;
- gain confidence in your ability to succeed in marriage; and
- accept that no one is perfect, yet we can still be terrific marriage partners.

# List # 1

A. List ten specific qualities you want in your spouse.
Review your list. Note whether each feature on it is something you want (W) or need (N). For example, you may think you need him to have a specific occupation, height, weight, or hair color. In general, desirable character traits are needs. Physical or material characteristics are more likely to be wants, which are less crucial than needs.

B. Did you include on your list some or all of these key traits for lasting happiness listed below?
  • kindness
  • empathy
  • sense of humor
  • chemistry
  • similar values
  • emotional stability
  • religious/spiritual compatibility
  • intellectual compatibility

   What other qualities do you consider essential in a husband?

C. Revise your list to include more needs and fewer wants. Is a vital trait missing? If so, add it to your list and remove a nonessential quality. It can help to discuss and evaluate your list with a wise person you trust, like a happily married friend, therapist, or another advisor.

D. You can rate the importance of each quality you've listed on a scale of one to ten, ten meaning most necessary, one meaning least needed.

## List # 2

Identify ten traits of your own that your future spouse is likely to appreciate. Keep your list in mind while you experience the ups and downs of dating, knowing that you deserve and can create a great marriage.

Instead of feeling like a beggar at a banquet, think of what you can offer. You are bringing your unique contributions, and some of them will complement those of your future partner.

## List # 3

A. List five less-than-perfect qualities in yourself, areas in which you have room to grow.

B. Remember that we can't expect to find a spouse who is perfect because no one is.

C. Recognize that the field of potential spouses has now significantly expanded.

## Lists Are Helpful but Not the Final Word

These lists are likely to be helpful, but they're not cast in stone. You may meet or already know someone who could be a suitable life partner, even if he lacks a quality or two on your list.

No one gets everything they want in life. But by thinking through what you want, need, and have to offer, and by recognizing your imperfections, you're on your way to creating a marriage that fulfills you emotionally and spiritually as well as physically and materially.

# LOVE

Every society in the world praises the value of love. Love takes us beyond self-centeredness and motivates us to connect meaningfully with one another. Yet, too often, the secular ideal of love emphasizes *being loved* or *receiving love*.

The Hebrew word for love —*ahavah*—includes the Aramaic word *hav*, which means "give." The initial letter *alef* makes it mean, "*I* will give." Loving is not so much receiving as giving of oneself and sacrificing for others.[1]

Romantic novels, movies, and fairy tales give a false idea about love. They glorify love at first sight, which rarely leads to a fulfilling marriage because it's usually based on fantasy. Yes, some couples fell in love right away, married quickly, and it worked out fine. However, Allison's experience is more common.

## Allison's Story

Allison, in her mid-twenties, looks like a breezy blond cover girl. She met Jim on a dating site, then in person. She was so charmed by him that instead of sensibly limiting their first date to a couple of hours, she agreed to a six-hour round-trip drive to a scenic location.

Allison and Jim left early in the day. They returned to her place at around one in the morning, exhausted, and she agreed to share her bed with him without sex. Their following two dates did include sex. Allison was in love—but with a fantasy. He loved sex, not her. When their relationship quickly turned into Jim texting her to hook up, she was devastated.

Had she known the difference between sex and love, Allison could have prevented feeling victimized.

## How Not to Fall Crazy in Love

Many of us can relate to Allison's story because it's easy to fantasize when we first meet someone. Before we know what he's like, it's easy to fill in the unknown with what we hope is there. Have you noticed yourself doing this? Do you think it's natural to fall in love quickly? Some women believe that they shouldn't suppress what happens naturally. But if you're looking for a lasting, fulfilling relationship, why set yourself up for disappointment?

Many women, like Allison, become involved too quickly. They confuse sex with love. Hormones have a way of doing that. Such women may believe the relationship is serious, and then they find out that the man wants no-strings-attached sex. They may continue to repeat their mistake in future relationships and become cynical about men and marriage because it never works out.

Before thinking about physical intimacy, a wise woman learns what type of relationship both she and a man want. If he says he hopes to marry, instead of rushing to the bedroom, she takes her time to learn if they're likely to be compatible in the long run and to see if she likes the real him: his values, interests, strengths, weaknesses—his endearing traits and his less appealing ones.

## What True Love Looks Like

Arlyn's parents showed her what real love looks like. "They were always there for each other," she says. "What I learned from my dad was to be nice to one's spouse. When she came downstairs dressed up but late, he didn't criticize her for being late to go out with him. He'd say, 'Oh, Mollye, you look lovely.' He always complimented her."

"Not that they never argued," Arlen adds. "Sometimes they'd snap at each other. Like when they came home from playing bridge. One might say to the other, 'I can't believe you played that card.' But it was always a love story. They knew every relationship has ups and downs, but they were always there for each other."

A widely respected spiritual leader, the Lubavitcher Rebbe, Menachem Mendel Schneerson, explains that what you read in novels isn't what happens in real life. "It's not as if two people meet and there is a sudden, blinding storm of passion. That's not what love or life is, or should be about." Instead, he said, "Two people meet and there might be a glimmer of understanding, like a tiny flame. And then, as these people decide to build a home together and go through the everyday activities and daily tribulations of life, this little flame grows even brighter and develops into a much bigger flame until these two people . . . become intertwined to such a point that neither of them can think of life without the other . . ."[2] He said, "It's the small acts that you do on a daily basis that turn two people from a 'you and I' into an 'us.'"[3]

# LOVE YOURSELF

*Love yourself first, and everything else falls into line. You really have to love yourself to get anything done in this world.*
—LUCILLE BALL

The idea that you need to love yourself before you can love someone else may sound paradoxical. The previous entry, Love, says that true love is about giving, not taking. Does that mean that self-love is selfish?

Not at all. Loving yourself empowers you to love another. Imagine yourself holding a cup filled to the brim with love. You have plenty of warmth, kindness, and caring to share with others.

But what if you've given and given while neglecting yourself for so long that your love cup is empty? You feel drained and numb. By being so "unselfish," you've become depleted and have nothing good to share.

## How to Love Yourself

So we need to keep refilling our love cup, which means making sure we care for ourselves in order to continue as a loving relationship partner.

*Love* is a verb. We display love, not so much by saying, "I love you," as by showing consideration and empathy. You show love for yourself by

- caring for yourself—your feelings and needs—as much as you care for another;
- maintaining healthy boundaries; and
- doing things that make you happy.

By keeping your love cup filled, you'll know that you are capable, appealing, and deserving of love. You become ready to accept, respect, and love an excellent relationship partner.

## Exercise

List at least five ways you show love for yourself.

# M is for

- Marriage
- Marriage Meetings
- Mentors
- Millennials
- Money: How Do You Relate to It?
- Money and Dating
- Money and Marriage

## MARRIAGE

*A successful marriage requires falling in love
many times, always with the same person.*
—Mignon McLaughlin

If you view marriage as a journey, you're more likely to succeed. People who see it as a destination are in store for a letdown. When the excitement fades, they wonder, *How could I have married this person?*

That thought can surface in any marriage.

I remember meeting a widower in his eighties when I was single and naive enough to think a relationship had to feel okay all the time or it wasn't worth keeping. His expression was radiant as he talked about his late wife: "Sometimes I thought she was an awful person. Other times, I thought she was so wonderful that I was blessed to be with her."

## All of Us Can Be Annoying

Estelle Reiner, the wife of the comedian, actor, director, and writer Carl Reiner for nearly sixty-five years, until her death in 2008, gives sage advice: "Marry someone who can stand you at your worst."

Her husband agreed that their long marriage was successful in part because they were able to stand each other. He said, "That's absolutely true! There are many, many reasons to break up, but if you can stand the worst of what they do, why break up? You're only going to get someone who will annoy you in another way so whatever little annoyances there are, you can stand that. We were able to stand each other very, very well."[1]

No one is lovable all the time.

When we were single, my friends and I talked about what was wrong with men, blithely unaware of our own shortcomings. In real-life good marriages, not the fairy-tale version, annoyances happen. Spouses who are compatible *and* realistic treasure each other regardless.

The idea is not to marry a man who loves, loves, loves you. It's to marry someone who will also stay the course when you're not so lovable. And to marry someone whom you'll still hold dear even when he slips up.

On a similar note, Rabbi Joseph Richards quips: "People are annoying. So find the person who annoys you the least and marry that one!"

Many spouses find that some of their partner's annoying traits are what attracted them at first. A wife who initially valued her husband's easygoing, calm nature later feels frustrated when he forgets to follow through with a chore. A husband initially liked how stylish his wife looked when they were first dating. Now he complains that she spends too much on clothes.

If you view marriage as a journey, you'll know that all marriages have ups and downs. We create a realistic version of happily ever after by learning to manage our differences with understanding and respect.

## Marriage Can Be the Ultimate Growth Experience

Viewing marriage as a journey means knowing it takes energy to keep the relationship thriving. You can put into place a simple routine that keeps the two of you reconnecting regularly: hold a weekly marriage meeting, as described below.

When you treat marriage as a journey, the glow will keep returning. You'll find it hard to imagine life without your mate. Learning to accept and appreciate differences, communicate positively and constructively, and behave in ways that bring out the best in yourself and your partner contribute to marriage as a growth experience. It takes some maturity to succeed in marriage; partners develop more of it by accepting each other as they are.

It makes sense to view marriage as a journey, not as the fixed moment of marrying but as an ever-changing reality as we grow through life's changes.

# MARRIAGE MEETINGS

By holding a weekly marriage meeting before and after marrying, you'll gain a simple way to keep your relationship flourishing.

Regardless of life's ups and downs, the two of you can increase intimacy, teamwork, and romance. You'll deal with issues constructively and create win-win solutions.

## What's a Marriage Meeting?

A marriage meeting is a short, gentle conversation. Couples meet alone once a week in a quiet place free from distractions. The meeting has a simple, loosely structured four-part agenda:

1. Express appreciation to each other.
2. Coordinate chores and responsibilities.
3. Plan for good times together as a couple, such as dates and vacations.
4. Address problems and challenges using positive communication skills.

I've been teaching this program to couples and therapists for over twenty years. Follow-up studies of spouses who continued to hold the meetings after participating in one of my workshops show that virtually all of them gained a significant increase in marital happiness.

I practice what I preach. My husband and I began holding weekly meetings during our first year of marriage and continue to do so more than thirty years later. I give them major credit for our lasting happiness.

## Benefits of Marriage Meetings

My book *Marriage Meetings for Lasting Love: 30 Minutes a Week to the Relationship You've Always Wanted* gives step-by-step instructions for holding the meetings. Couples who conduct them effectively resolve conflicts more smoothly. If your marriage is already good, the meetings will keep it thriving. If you are facing unusual challenges, they can help the two of you deal with them well.

By following this program, couples also create a safe forum to air grievances or bring up sticky subjects, such as sex, money, parenting concerns, in-law relationships, or other matters. The positive communication skills useful for marriage meetings also help relate to family members, friends, coworkers, and others.

## Marriage Meetings Are Proactive

Marriage meetings prevent crises because they encourage couples to deal with small frustrations constructively. By addressing concerns promptly, we clear up misunderstandings and prevent grudge holding.

A psychologist in a class I taught for therapists said, "The happiest couple I know has been holding a weekly meeting for fifty years."

Some couples find that they can communicate effectively without the routine after conducting marriage meetings for a while. Some hold meetings less often than weekly. I think weekly is best for staying on course because spouses make sure to regularly give and receive appreciation, handle chores smoothly, schedule a weekly date, and promptly resolve issues. So unfinished business is less likely to cloud the relationship.

For a small investment of time, the rewards are enormous. So discuss the idea of holding marriage meetings with a potential spouse when your relationship is becoming committed—or with your spouse after you've married.

### When to Conduct Your First Marriage Meeting

If you're able to start holding meetings before the wedding, you'll be off to a good start for making them a habit. But it's never too late to begin.

# MENTORS

If you were blessed with parents who got along well, you probably learned much, as though by osmosis, about how to create a good marriage. Your live-in mentors paved the way.

But what if your parents stayed together unhappily or divorced? Or what if you were raised by a single parent? Typically, couples who see me for therapy grew up without viewing a healthy marriage. For them and others who yearn for a fulfilling, lasting union, mentoring can help fill the gaps.

Even if your parents were happy together, their way might not be your way. Today, the most fulfilling marriages tend to be more egalitarian and collaborative than the kind some of us saw as children. Also, more flexibility in gender roles occurs now regarding income-earning and homemaking responsibilities.

## Adopting Realistic Expectations

A good mentor helps you form realistic beliefs about marriage. I needed this sort of help. My parents divorced when I was thirteen. My mother's friends were unhappily married, divorced, or single.

I learned from fairy tales and romantic novels that all you have to do is find a perfect man to fall in love with, marry him, and then live happily ever after. Then, with absolutely no effort on your part, he'll do everything you want without your having to say a word because he's so good at reading your mind, and you'll have a perfect marriage.

When an imperfection surfaced in a man I was dating, I stopped seeing him. I pined after men I viewed as perfect. I thought I was in love, but I loved a fantasy because I barely knew the person, his strengths and weaknesses.

For many years this pattern kept me from marrying. I complained to my friends about how sad it was that the men I liked didn't want to commit. Finally, I realized that I feared marriage. Hadn't it ruined the lives of my mother and some of her friends?

I was expressing my conflict about marrying by choosing men who were not suitable for me.

My mentors helped me transform from a commitment-phobic woman to a happily married one. Some of them don't know that they helped me because mentoring can be subtle. It could be an offhand remark or advice from someone who doesn't know you took it.

You may have expectations of marriage that are not realistic. You may think you'll need to do it all—hold a stressful job, run a household, and be there for your husband and children. A good mentor can help you define your priorities and make adjustments to keep you sane.

## Finding Good Role Models

As a young adult, I found mentors among friends and colleagues. Here are a couple of examples:

A friend told me, "The best time for me to talk to my husband about something sensitive is when we're in bed after we've had sex." Maybe that's not the best time for everyone. But it makes sense to talk about a touchy topic when both of you are likely to be receptive. For some couples, right after sex might be okay; for others, it might be a different time, like when neither of you is tired, hungry, or stressed.

When I was a child welfare worker in San Francisco, Emily, a young married coworker, told me, as noted in the Introduction, "You don't marry a prince charming; you make him one by how you treat him."

## Developing Realistic Expectations

When I was the executive director of a family service agency, I gained a mentor who served on its board of directors. Linda, a happily married physician, had two small children. She said about her husband, "I'm not in love with him; I'm very *fond* of him."

Wow! Fond? Not madly in love? That was a new concept for me. I suppose "in love" means different things to different people, so it may be a matter of semantics. But I learned that liking someone and being comfortable being myself with him was much more important than having the crazy-in-love feeling, and I mean *crazy*, because confusing that state with true love is a big mistake.

I was excited and somewhat dazed after becoming engaged. But I enjoyed David's company while staying grounded instead of losing myself by getting swept into a fantasy.

## Mentors Are Plentiful

In case you're wondering where to find mentors, here are some ideas:

- at your synagogue, church, or another place of worship
- in groups or organizations

- at work
- among happily married friends, relatives, and acquaintances
- in a therapist or other professional counselor

You can find mentors just about anywhere. Notice couples who laugh and enjoy each other. You can learn from them.

Here's a simple example of how a therapist can serve as a mentor who helps you replace marriage myths with more realistic expectations:

> When a wife says she's frustrated because her husband doesn't talk about his feelings, I'd probably empathize. But I might also say that most men find it harder than women to express emotions. When she hears this, she's likely to start accepting her husband as normal instead of judging him as cold, withholding, or unfeeling. When she becomes more compassionate toward her husband, he's more likely to feel safe enough to express his feelings.

## Mentors Want You to Succeed

Your mentors are on your team. They want you to succeed and be happy.

### *Exercise:*

1. If you already have marriage mentors, list them. Next to each one, write what you're learning from them.
2. If you want a marriage mentor, think about where you might find one. Write down your ideas.

# MILLENNIALS

Is dating different for millennials than for other age groups? Actually, yes and no. The answer depends mainly on how a millennial decides to approach dating.

The Pew Research Center defines millennials as people born between 1981 and 1996. If you're one of them, you may approach romantic love differently from people of earlier generations. Most millennials rely heavily on technology. The endless array of dating apps and choices can make it difficult to commit to a relationship. It becomes especially challenging to balance the desire for independence with commitment needs.

Communication mishaps abound for millennials because text messages have largely replaced phone calls. We may think that our choice of words determines the bulk of a personal message people receive. As noted earlier, body language, which is absent from text messages, accounts for 55 percent of what's understood. Voice tone, which expresses 38 percent of the meaning, is present in phone conversations and is missing from texts.[2]

What's more, technology can dehumanize us. It easily removes the constraints that usually exist in ordinary interactions where there is a shared respect for each other's humanity. When communication is mainly online and therefore more superficial, it becomes easier to "ghost" someone, to disappear with no explanation, rather than have a respectful conversation. Ghosting has become a common way to end an online relationship.

Being ghosted can hurt someone who thought she was in a real relationship. Because technology can foster emotional distance, the "ghost" may forget that he's dealing with a real human being who deserves a kinder sort of goodbye than a disappearance.

Millennials tend to go with the crowd. Yet it's essential to recognize the temptation to do what others are doing. Instead, say no to what doesn't feel okay to you. It's best to meet and date people in a way that fits your unique self.

Although online dating has become enormously popular, marriages also occur when people first meet in person at an event or through a friend, relative, or matchmaking service. Millennials in college or graduate school have a fairly easy time meeting new people. Many spouses in successful marriages met as students. Of course, you can sign up for a class that interests you at any age or stage of life. You never know who you might meet there.

## Avoiding Online Dating Hazards

Although disappointments occur in online dating, they can happen regardless of how two people first meet, especially if our happily-ever-after fantasies soar before we know someone well. While online dating has challenges, it can also be gratifying. About one-third of recent marriages began with an online introduction.

Here are a few suggestions for a positive online dating experience:

- Before meeting in person, try to learn if his description of himself is honest. Is he really single? Did he state his age truthfully? Some people will ask for references. Many balk at this idea but find what they want to know via social media.
- Do not prolong an online relationship beyond when you're ready to speak by phone or meet in person.
- If the person will communicate only online (texting, sending emails, etc.) well past the time when you're ready to talk on the phone or meet in person, this is a *virtual* relationship. Say goodbye and find a real one.

## Dating Advice for Millennials

"Dating used to be more respectful," says Gina, thirty-three, a married bank executive. "These days, people get involved too quickly," she says. "They become a couple before they really know each other, and it doesn't last because they've rushed into things too soon, and then they end up breaking up." Gina advises millennials to take time to get to know each other and how they behave over time. Learn about his interests. Get to know his family. If you've come to know his fine points and you want to stay with him, you'll stay in the relationship even as you go through the ups and downs.

Gina knew her husband well and his family too before marrying eight years ago. She exudes calm happiness when she talks about her marriage and her two young children.

Gina's advice is sound. She agrees that dating for a millennial is pretty much like dating for women of other generations. It makes sense to notice whether someone you date has the traits you need in a husband. If you think the two of you might be moving toward commitment, clarify whether he wants an exclusive relationship with you or if he's still keeping his options open. Maintain your objectivity by devoting no more of yourself to a relationship than the person you're dating does.

Texting is fine for confirming an appointment time or other facts. Hold emotionally charged conversations in person or on the phone.

## Francie's Take on Millennial Men

Francie, single and in her late twenties, echoes Gina's view that dating is less respectful than it used to be. She says, "Men want to meet you for coffee or a drink. If they ask for another date, they want to meet you for coffee or at a bar. They don't want to go for dinner; it's too expensive because they go out with so many women."

Yet if a woman is emotionally healthy and ready for marriage, she'll attract marriage-minded men who want to get to know her as a person rather than as one of many women they date in rapid succession.

Sincerity attracts sincerity. If you are comfortable with yourself and confident that you are on a path toward marriage, you will attract men with a similar mindset. The players will go elsewhere on their own, or you'll send them on their way.

# MONEY

Money is a sensitive subject for most of us. Who isn't a little bit weird about money, anyway? The topic of money in dating and marriage is filled with ambiguity and a wealth (ahem) of possible answers. The subject can fill an entire book, and it does. (See Reading List, page 222.) The next three entries address money issues:

- Money: How Do You Relate to It?
- Money and Dating
- Money and Marriage

# MONEY: HOW DO YOU RELATE TO IT?

Early in our lives, we pick up lasting ideas about money, mostly from our parents or parental figures. My parents felt fortunate to begin their New York City public school teaching careers during the Great Depression in the 1930s when people who'd lost everything were selling apples on the street.

Although I was well provided for while growing up, I picked up these unspoken messages from my parents about money:

- Talking about money is not okay.
- Asking for money is certainly not okay.
- It's okay to accept money when it's offered.
- A gift of money means the giver loves me.
- Saving is good.
- It's best to buy only things that you can pay for in full at the time.
- Make sure you can support yourself in case your husband leaves.

How people deal with money in a relationship can bring about strong feelings. We may feel more loved, less loved, or unloved, depending on whether a man spends money on us or withholds it. Or other feelings may arise.

## Money as Love

"He (or she) doesn't love me" or "doesn't appreciate me" is a feeling that can occur when we think a man we're involved with isn't being generous enough.

According to a survey by Ramsey Solutions, "money fights are the second leading cause of divorce, behind infidelity. Results show that both high levels of debt and a lack of communication are major causes for the stress and anxiety surrounding household finances."[3]

Often, the real issue behind a conflict about money involves how spouses feel about each other and their relationship. These emotions can easily spill over into how they address concerns about money. (See Money and Marriage, page 104.)

## Money as Power

Some people use money as a way to try to control a relationship partner; some use it as a way to avoid being controlled by one. An insecure man might spend more on a date than he can afford, hoping a woman will feel obliged to go out with him again.

Some women insist on paying for themselves on a date because they don't want to feel controlled. Others let the man treat them on a first date but make sure it's just for coffee because they'd feel guilty if a man spends a lot on dinner. They don't want to feel like they owe something in return, such as physical intimacy or another date.

I'm concerned about women looking for a man mainly for financial support because they're setting themselves up for a power imbalance. An ironic version of the Golden Rule states, "Remember the Golden Rule: Whoever has the gold makes the rules!"

A power imbalance can develop when the husband is the breadwinner and the wife cannot support herself financially. I advise women who want an equal partnership to become financially self-sufficient. Those who know they can take care of themselves economically are in a good position to create a collaborative relationship between two adults, which is the best kind.

*Dinner Date*

## Money as Security

People who view money as a source of security want to be ready for the future. They'll save for a vacation, a car, a down payment on a home, or retirement. They want a cushion to fall back on in case of a job loss or other unexpected costly event.

## Money as a Means of Instant Gratification

Opposite of savers are people like George—thirty-eight and single. He lived in a rented apartment in an upscale building in a prime San Francisco location, near the café where he ate his daily croissant-and-latte breakfast. He didn't have to order because the servers knew his routine. He ate breakfast, lunch, and often dinner at restaurants.

George owned a successful business but lived hand to mouth. He said, "I'd like to treat my parents to a week's vacation in Hawaii, but I don't have the money."

People who want to save money are more likely to prepare most of their meals, eat out less often, or spend less on other things. They think building a nest egg is more important than spending in ways they consider wasteful.

Answering the questions in the exercise below can help you to identify your attitudes about money and the source of your thoughts and feelings about it. There are no right or wrong responses. As we gain self-understanding, we're more likely to handle money situations more smoothly when dating or married.

## Exercise: How Do You View Money?

1. What kinds of conversations about money, if any, occurred in your family while you were growing up?
2. What spoken or unspoken rule(s) about money existed in your family?
3. Which of the above rules influence how you deal with money now, and how?
4. Are you a saver, a spender, or both?

5. What does it mean to you when a potential or actual partner
   - spends money on you? (Do you feel loved? Obligated, guilty, or entitled? Something else?)
   - withholds spending money on you?
   - expects you to pay your "fair" share?

# MONEY AND DATING

*The way I see it, the guy should ALWAYS pay for the first date, just to even things out. Have you been inside a Sephora? An eye shadow palette is about 45 bucks—that's five times the price of mozzarella sticks.*

—The Captain@sgrstk (tweeted)

Who pays on dates? It used to be simple. The guy did the asking and the paying. Today it's less clear, as we can see from the range of views on the topic:

- **Tom**, twenty-six, says he paid for the first five or six dates with his girlfriend of three years, who's twenty-nine. "She felt bad about me always paying, so sometimes she does. But I usually pay," he says. "And the guy is always expected to pay for the first date. I pay more because it's the gentlemanly thing to do. If you're a guy, it feels good to take a woman out to dinner."
- **Marge**, thirty-five, liked being treated on her first few dates with Wesley. They quickly became involved romantically and sexually. Marge said that on a later date, he asked her to go on a picnic. "I was behind him on the line to pick up sandwiches and drinks. He paid for his and left me to pay for mine. I felt awful."

    Wesley, it turned out, wanted a hookup relationship. Did he set Marge up to buy her own lunch to show that he didn't want to connect meaningfully with her? It felt like that to her.

- **Brandon**, sixty-nine, on the other hand, said that while dating, he and the woman he later married always split the cost. "I thought that was fair; she was doing the right thing."
- **Teresa**, forty-five and married for two years, said that when she and her husband were dating, "he always asked, and he always paid," and "that was fine with both of us." She mused, "I've heard that there was more sharing the cost in the 1960s and '70s."
- **Penny**, fifty-one, in an off-guard moment, mentioned that she always expects the guy to pay and mumbled something about her father having abandoned her family when she was young.

## So Who Should Pay?

Most agree that the man pays for the first date and often for the next few. But after that, it's anybody's guess. If you have a strong preference for who should pay, you can initiate a calm conversation in which each of you shares how you'd like to handle the financial part of dating.

If you feel shy about bringing up the subject, you're not alone. My family's "don't ask for money" rule stayed with me, unconsciously, into adulthood. So it was difficult for me to talk about money on dates. I wanted the man to treat me, even if I offered to pay, which I sometimes felt obliged to do. Wasn't I a feminist? Didn't that mean I should pay my way? I expected the man to read my mind because I was embarrassed to let him know I wanted him to treat me.

## Can a Feminist Let a Man Treat Her?

When I offered to split the check on a dinner date, I felt unfeminine if the man accepted, which meant no second date. I thought he was cheap or didn't like me very much. But now, I think many men were as confused as I was. They might have thought I wanted to pay my way. Maybe they feared I'd reject them as sexist if they refused my offer.

Most people would probably agree that the splitting-the-bill trend has subsided. These days, men usually pay for early dates. Many, or possibly most men, seem prepared to continue to pay, but as the relationship evolves, they may be open to sharing some expenses if offered.

When my husband-to-be asked me out for the first time, I told him that I'd already planned to see a play on my own that Saturday night, which was true. He said he'd like to go with me, not "take me," which created ambiguity about whether this would be a real date. I asked, "Are you planning to treat?" Fortunately, he said yes.

I learned that feminism means being myself, regardless of what others are doing.

How about you? Answering the questions below may help clarify your views about money as it relates to dating.

## Exercise: Identifying Your Views on Money and Dating

1. Do you expect the man to pay for the first date? What are your thoughts about this?
2. Who do you think should pay for subsequent dates?
3. How do you feel when a man spends money on you? Do you sometimes feel guilty or obligated? Sense a power imbalance? Accept it graciously? Enjoy feeling feminine? Or something else? Please explain.
4. Under what circumstances do you feel inclined to share expenses or reciprocate, after a man spends money on you initially or over time?
5. How comfortable are you about sharing your ideas and feelings with a man about dating's financial aspects?
6. Did you get the impression while growing up that men should treat you on dates, that you should pay your way, or something else?
7. Has your thinking about dating and money changed since then? If yes, how is it different now?

# MONEY AND MARRIAGE

When your relationship becomes serious, make sure to talk about how you're going to deal with money when you're married. Who will pay the rent or mortgage? Electricity, vacations, entertainment, and so on?

Will each of you have discretionary money, an amount you can spend on whatever you wish without having to justify such purchases? Or will you need to agree on where every dollar goes? Will you collaborate regarding money decisions? Or will one of you, explicitly or implicitly, be in charge of finances?

Although we cannot anticipate every contingency, here are a few more questions to consider:

- Will you have a joint checking account or credit card(s), separate ones, or both?
- If you have a joint account, who puts how much money into it and when?
- Will you hold savings accounts and other funds individually or jointly?
- Will both of you earn income by working?
- If a baby arrives, will one of you be a stay-at-home parent? How might your approach to financial matters change?
- What income, savings, and investments do each of you have?

The more you clarify in advance about finances, the fewer unwelcome surprises are likely to come. So state your feelings, wants, and needs about money constructively, first to yourself and then to your partner, as calmly and confidently as you can.

## Andrea's Story: Saying What You Need

While it's not easy for many of us to discuss money with a marriage partner, it's vital to do so to prevent misunderstandings that can result in future conflicts.

Andrea and her husband, Louis, are both thirty-eight, and they talked about money before marrying. They agreed on how much of each of their incomes would go into a joint checking account. They decided to keep their separate assets, acquired while single, in their own names. Louis and Andrea agreed that she would quit her job to be a full-time mom.

All was fine until after their baby arrived. Andrea loved being home with the baby. But when she realized that she wasn't going to return to work for several years, she began to feel uneasy about the growing difference between her and her husband's net worth. While Louis was increasing his savings and retirement accounts, she could no longer add to hers.

Andrea tried to share her uneasy feelings about this with Louis a couple of times. He dismissed them, saying she had nothing to worry about.

She feared he would think she was greedy if she mentioned her concern again. She felt some shame and thought it might be petty to dwell on financial "unfairness" when, all in all, she had a beautiful life and a great husband.

So she stopped trying to talk to him about her feelings about their money situation. Consequently, she began feeling distant from him. *He doesn't love me*, she thought. Her resentment increased because of his "insensitivity."

Finally, she and Louis saw a therapist together. During the session, Andrea talked about her insecurities related to her parents' divorce when she was twelve. She hoped her marriage would last but wanted a financial cushion, just in case.

Louis murmured about women who divorced their husbands and wiped them out financially. *He's frightened too*, Andrea realized.

In the safety of the therapy office, they gained empathy for each other. They recognized that they were both committed to their marriage. During the session, Andrea fearfully asked for what she wanted, which was for Louis to contribute some of his income each month to her separate savings account. Louis agreed to her request, and both were satisfied.

## Is the Conflict about Money or Something Else?

Although conflicts about money and sex are often cited as causes of divorce, the real issue is likely to be the spouses' failure to communicate their wants and needs about money, sex, or something else.

Money can represent love, power, or security. Can you see how money means all three for Andrea? What do you think money represents for Louis?

As the above example shows, it is not the money itself that causes conflict in a marriage, but a lack of understanding about our own and our partner's attitudes regarding it. Andrea and Louis could deal with their conflict constructively by becoming aware of each other's thoughts, feelings, and needs about money.

## How to Talk about Money

When considering how to talk about money in dating and marriage, three main topics are relevant: fairness, feelings, and beliefs.

### Fairness

How do we decide what's fair concerning money? If he earns twice as much as you, should he pay twice as much toward expenses? What if you make more?

If you're married, should you and your partner share all money each of you earns? If one of you quits her or his job to take on the bulk of parenting or homemaking responsibilities, does the breadwinner get to make the financial decisions? What might it cost to pay someone to do all the tasks now being done by the spouse who may have sacrificed or postponed a career?

What if one partner enters the marriage with significantly more assets, which might legally remain that person's separate property forever, depending on the law in your state or country?

A husband who grew up in a patriarchal culture may think it's fair for him to make significant financial decisions, even if he's not the primary breadwinner. If his wife disagrees, she may argue futilely or become secretive about her spending. When either partner withdraws instead of talking about difficult feelings, resentment is likely to grow and, consequently, the relationship will suffer.

## Feelings

If you want a loving and caring marriage, avoid dwelling on what's fair because that tends to cause fruitless arguments. Instead, calmly and respectfully, say what you need to feel loved and secure and hear what your partner's needs are too. (See Communication, page 22.)

## Beliefs

By identifying your own and your partner's beliefs about money, you'll lay the groundwork for constructive discussions. Here are a few examples of assumptions, which may not be conscious but can affect marital relationships:

- A wife believes both partners should agree on all major expenses; her husband thinks otherwise.
- A husband believes he needs to keep his wife financially dependent on him. The wife thinks she should not need to account for every penny spent.
- A wife thinks her husband should be the breadwinner and she should be a homemaker. He views women with no outside-of-home interests as dull or clingy.
- A wife feels okay about earning more than her easygoing husband; she thinks his personality balances her intense nature well. He finds her exciting.

Spouses in the first three of the above examples have conflicting beliefs about money. The fourth example shows a couple with compatible views about money.

Let's look at how each couple's relationship is affected by their beliefs about money.

*Example A. A wife believes both partners should agree on all major expenses; her husband thinks otherwise.*

Anna assumed that her husband, Cal, shared her belief. So she was shocked when, without consulting her, he paid more to replace a car's transmission than the car was worth. His view was, "It's my car. I drive it, and I want to keep it." Anna found his attitude frustrating. She told him that from then on, she'd like for them to agree about significant expenses. Cal hemmed and hawed. Anna wasn't sure he'd act differently in the future but was glad she expressed her feelings.

*Example B. A husband believes he needs to keep his wife financially dependent on him. The wife thinks she should not need to account for every penny spent.*

After they married, Jolene moved into Parker's apartment, which was close to his job. Because Jolene's commute to her lower-paying job was exhausting, they agreed that she would quit, but they failed to discuss in advance how they would deal with money after she was no longer earning any.

Parker turned out to be possessive about "his" money and didn't give her enough for basics like groceries. After their baby was born, Jolene wanted to get a part-time job. Parker said no; the baby needed her. Jolene's resentment grew. Finally, she moved in with her mother, who helped care for the baby while she worked.

*Example C. A wife thinks her husband should be the breadwinner and she should be a homemaker. He views women with no outside-of-home interests as dull or clingy.*

Katharine was fifty-four when she married Harvey, who was sixty-three. After decades of holding high-stress, creative jobs, Katharine decided to be a homemaker. She liked organizing their place and cooking elaborate meals. When Harvey arrived home, she wanted to hear all about his day, but she had nothing to say about hers. He wondered what happened to the vibrant woman he married, whom he expected to continue working.

Ten years later, Harvey routinely works late. He's been wanting a divorce for years but feels social pressure to stay married. Katharine suspects infidelity.

**Example D.** (compatible beliefs about money) *A wife feels okay about earning more than her easygoing husband; she thinks his personality balances her intense nature well. He finds her exciting.*

Gina, fifty, a highly successful software engineer, thrives in her work for technology start-up companies. Her husband, Ralph, fifty-seven, likes being a librarian. Their salaries and Gina's bonuses go into joint accounts. They agree on major purchasing decisions.

During their twenty-five years of marriage, Gina has consistently out-earned Ralph. Both are happy with how things worked out.

## Exercise: Money and Marriage

1. Is one of the above examples (A, B, C, or D) of spouses' beliefs about money and marriage similar to your situation?
2. The first three examples show how conflicting beliefs can stress a marriage. How might each couple have prevented the discord that developed between them?
3. Were you advised to keep a stash of your own money for security after marrying because you never know what might happen?
4. Make a list of specific money concerns to discuss when a relationship becomes serious.

a. _____

b. _____

c. _____

d. _____

e. _____

f. _____

# N is for

o **Negotiate**
o **No**

## NEGOTIATE

Before marriage, many people don't talk about what's important to them or address differences. They think some version of "We're so in love, nothing bad can happen to our relationship." But then they get married, and life sets in. Expectations that may have been unconscious can surface in many areas. They can stress your relationship to the point where you start thinking about ending it.

In a successful relationship, partners foster harmony by being aware of their own and each other's needs and talking about them kindly and respectfully. Some people are afraid to express their true feelings about an issue because they fear that doing so will upset their partner or make him or her uncomfortable. But if you hold back, it won't be good for your relationship.

Negotiation in a healthy relationship involves two people who relate as equals, who sometimes have different wants, needs, and expectations. It's important to recognize differences. Some of them probably attracted you to each other initially, yet these same qualities can cause conflict later.

Depending on your particular situation, I cannot overemphasize the importance of discussing and agreeing on most or all of these potential minefields before committing to marriage:

- How will we organize our finances? (See Money in Marriage, page 104.)
- How will we relate to in-laws, how often will we see them, and with whom will we spend various holidays? What kinds of boundaries might we want to establish? (See Boundaries, page 15.)
- What kind of parents do we want to be? What values do we want to instill, including religious identity? How will we relate to stepchildren or a former spouse?
- How will we spend our leisure time together and separately?
- Do you want to keep your current last name, adopt that of your husband-to-be, or do the two of you want to agree on something different?
- Where will we live?
- Will we hold weekly marriage meetings[1] to keep our relationship thriving? (See Marriage Meetings, page 88.)

## Rosie's Story

Rosie loves Gabe, who has proposed marriage. He wants her to quit her job and move to a distant city with him, where he's been offered a job. She says yes, although it flashes through her mind that she'll miss being near her family and friends. She'll have to quit a job she likes that pays well. But she says nothing about her doubts because she fears upsetting him.

Actually, by expressing her reservations, Rosie would be giving Gabe a gift. She would be making it possible for him to respond to her sensitively. He can't read her mind. If she doesn't share her thoughts and feelings, how can she expect him to consider them?

If Rosie silently goes along with his wishes by moving and becomes unhappy, she will likely feel victimized and resentful, and the relationship will suffer.

What if Rosie were to say to Gabe, "I'm not sure I'm ready to move. I like having my friends and family nearby, and I love my job." Suppose a happy marriage is more important to Gabe than moving to a faraway city with a resentful wife. In that case, he might well be willing to either stay put for the time being or to consider alternatives that both of them could accept.

Perhaps Rosie would be ready to move on a trial basis with the understanding that if she or he wants to move back in a year, then they will. If he has a job and she does not, perhaps they can agree on how they will handle finances if she is unemployed. Maybe in advance, they'll agree that she'll fly back to see friends and family regularly.

When both people are honest about their needs and can negotiate respectfully, a mutually satisfying solution often results.

## Using Positive Communication Skills

By using positive communication skills to express your feelings and preferences, you are more likely to meet your needs and strengthen your relationship. An emotionally healthy man wants to please you. It's your job to tell him how.

Rabbi Manis Friedman illustrates how negotiation occurs in an ideal marriage. The wife likes to sleep with the window open, and her husband wants it closed. Each wants the other to be comfortable. So she insists that the window stay closed because that's what he wants. He insists that it remain open because that's what she wants. Each has empathy for and wants the other to be happy.

So what do they end up doing? They might ask each other, "On a scale of one to ten, how strong is your wish to have the window the way you want it?" and then decide accordingly.

This kind of relating reflects a high level of empathy. Nevertheless, negotiating isn't about treating one's partner as an enemy to overpower. Nor is it about placating by caving in. It is about having a back-and-forth, give-and-take discussion. It's about knowing that there can be joy in compromising and creating agreements that make both of you happy.

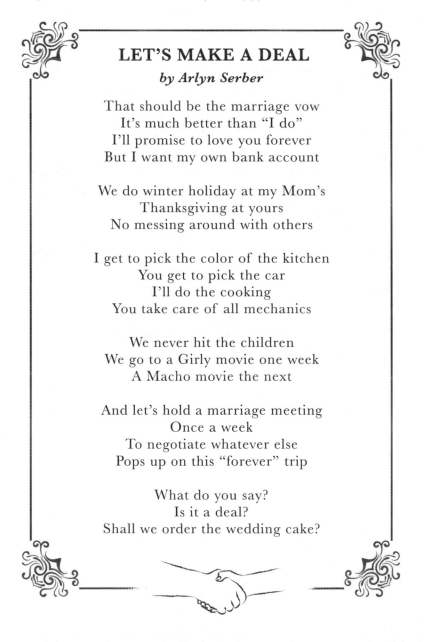

## LET'S MAKE A DEAL
### *by Arlyn Serber*

That should be the marriage vow
It's much better than "I do"
I'll promise to love you forever
But I want my own bank account

We do winter holiday at my Mom's
Thanksgiving at yours
No messing around with others

I get to pick the color of the kitchen
You get to pick the car
I'll do the cooking
You take care of all mechanics

We never hit the children
We go to a Girly movie one week
A Macho movie the next

And let's hold a marriage meeting
Once a week
To negotiate whatever else
Pops up on this "forever" trip

What do you say?
Is it a deal?
Shall we order the wedding cake?

# NO

Most of us want to be liked, which can cause us to say yes to someone or something when we'd be better off saying no. If you wish to marry, it's important to say no to relationships unlikely to move toward it.

Why spend precious time with someone who lacks the qualities you need in a husband or doesn't want to commit? There are many ways to say no to what doesn't suit you. People for whom saying no is new may start out saying it insensitively. For example, let's say that Louisa has just decided to stop being a people pleaser. When she's asked for a date by someone who doesn't interest her, she might answer with one word: "No." A kinder response would be, "Thank you very much. I appreciate you for asking me, but I don't think we're a good dating match."

Being clear and direct is important. Ideally, you'll say no pleasantly, but one way or another, do remember to say no to what's not right for you. By doing so, you'll make room to say yes to whom and what does fit for you.

You owe it to yourself to maintain healthy boundaries that support you toward reaching your goal.

# O is for

- ○ Online dating
- ○ Openness
- ○ Opposites

## ONLINE DATING

Some women still balk at the idea of meeting someone online. Yet between 2005 and 2012, one-third of all couples who got married in the United States met on the internet. By now, even more are probably meeting this way.[1]

Popular Los Angeles matchmaker Rena Hirsch recommends a three-pronged approach to finding someone to marry:

- Contact a matchmaker.
- Attend events where you can meet singles.
- Meet people online.

You'll increase your chances of finding someone compatible by first doing a bit of research. Some sites are clearly for people looking for marriage. Yet marriage can result from dating someone who doesn't spell out on a site that he wants it. There are sites for different religions, age groups, interests, and so on. A friend might help you create your profile or suggest a website. You can search online for names and types of dating sites.

Before meeting someone in person, do you want to make sure he's representing himself accurately? You may have heard a horror story about internet dating. How do you know if he's being truthful about his age, if his photo is from decades ago, or if it's of someone else? Is he married? Is he emotionally unstable?

We want to feel optimistic, not expect the worst. So it makes sense to prepare for a successful dating experience with someone you meet online. Many women say they'll check out someone by seeing how he presents himself on social media sites. They also get informal references while dating by meeting his friends and family members.

Meet for the first time in a public place for coffee or dessert. Keep your safety in mind before you know if this is someone you'll want to see again.

## If You See a Red Flag, Don't Ignore It

Ellie's experience shows why to notice red flags, especially with someone you meet online. Ellie didn't ask Stu for references. She was twenty-six and eager to marry. After a year of dating Stu, he took her shopping to look at engagement rings. She was ecstatic.

But instead of producing a ring, he disappeared with no explanation. While grieving the loss, Ellie wondered, *How could I have been so stupid? Who was this man?*

What was the real reason he'd never given her his phone number or let her come to his home? He'd implied that his occupation required much secrecy. Was he married? If she had paid attention to these red flags, she would have saved much time and avoided heartbreak.

## Happy Ending This Time

Gina and Milt, both in their early thirties, met online. Each had been disappointed by people they'd met on a dating site, and neither wanted another frustrating experience. It turned out that they already knew some of the same people who could vouch for Gina's and Milt's sincerity and trustworthiness. They've now been happily married for twelve years and have four children.

# OPENNESS

Openness is appealing. In a good relationship, you can share your genuine thoughts and feelings. This doesn't mean impulsively blurting out any stray thought or momentary emotion. It's best to communicate respectfully, express yourself with I-statements, and listen attentively. By being accepting and supportive, you nurture a relationship that grows in trust, caring, and admiration.

When you think about sharing something personal, it helps to begin with the end in mind. Ask yourself, "What do I hope will result?" Do you want to encourage a safe climate in which both of you feel free to express your true selves?

You might feel tempted to reveal very private information that could be a deal breaker, especially if shared too soon. Disclosure about things that could significantly affect your relationship should certainly happen before you commit to marriage. If you have children, it's fair to disclose this promptly because their presence can be a deal breaker for some.

But why mention significant debts or a physical or mental condition that is not obvious when you barely know someone? It makes sense to wait until he's learned over time that you're kind, fun to be with, hardworking, loyal, honest, bright, engaging, and so on. Be sensitive to the timing of sharing and its relevance to you as a couple. For more thoughts on this topic, see Secrets, page 143.

## When Hot Buttons Get Pushed

What if he asks you on a first date why you divorced, why you're still single, or some other question that feels too personal to answer honestly to someone you barely know? Respond pleasantly by letting him know it's a bit too soon for you to talk about something so private. You might imply that you've been learning a lot about yourself and growing as a person from your experiences. Or you can politely change the subject.

## Exercise

How much to open up is often a judgment call. To help decide whether or when to share, ask yourself these questions:

- How well do I know this person?
- Is he likely to gossip?
- Does he seem judgmental?
- How much private information about himself has he shared with me?
- What are the pros and cons of sharing a secret with him now?
- When is the best time to share my secret?

# OPPOSITES

News Flash! Just about everyone agrees opposites attract—but they don't. Many relationship experts write that people seek partners whose traits complement their own.

But it's a myth that opposites attract, states Matthew D. Johnson, chair & professor of psychology and director of the Marriage and Family Studies Laboratory, Binghamton University, State University of New York. Here's what he writes:

> Love stories often include people finding partners who seem to have traits that they lack, like a good girl falling for a bad boy. In this way, they appear to complement one another. For example, one spouse might be outgoing and funny, while the other is shy and serious. It's

easy to see how both partners could view the other as ideal—one partner's strengths balancing out the other partner's weaknesses. . . . The question is whether people actually seek out complementary partners or if that just happens in the movies.

As it turns out, it's pure fiction. There is essentially no research evidence that differences in personality, interests, education, politics, upbringing, religion, or other traits lead to greater attraction. . . .

Researchers have investigated what combination makes for better romantic partners—those who are similar, different, or opposite? . . . Social scientists have conducted over 240 studies to determine whether similarity in terms of *attitudes, personality traits, outside interests, values,* and *other characteristics* leads to attraction. In 2013, psychologists Matthew Montoya and Robert Horton examined the combined results of these studies in what's called a meta-analysis. They found an irrefutable association between being similar to and being interested in the other person.

In other words, there is clear and convincing evidence that birds of a feather flock together. For human beings, the attractiveness of similarity is so strong that it is found *across cultures.*[2]

Truths about arranged marriages support the case for similarities attracting. According to Utpal Dholakia, PhD, in Indian arranged marriages, "prospects come vetted." They are matched in characteristics such as social class, religion, caste (still today for Hindus), and educational attainment, which signals *similarity,* and such likenesses may be important predictors of longer-term marriage success.[3]

Marriage arrangers routinely pair people with similar values and lifestyles. Those in these marriages report high levels of satisfaction over the longer term. A study concludes that over time "the love experienced by Indian couples in arranged marriages appears to be even more robust than the love people experience in 'love marriages.'"[4]

## Why the "Opposites Attract" Myth Persists

Given all the evidence to the contrary, why does the myth that opposites attract persist? We may take our similarities for granted because they're not as obvious as our differences. Consequently, spouses may give more weight to differences like introverted/ extroverted, emotional/intellectual, planner/spontaneous person, and so on.

A way to make sense of this apparent contradiction is to differentiate between "opposite" and "different." The studies mentioned above conclude that similarities attract observable characteristics such as attitudes, personality traits, outside interests, and values—traits that reflect one's essential self.

The complementary dissimilarities, which may stand out in compatible couples, are secondary in importance to their essential similarities. Examples of such less significant contrasting traits are optimist/worrier, morning person/night person, and adventure seeker/security seeker. These differences are not deal breakers when they occur in a respectful relationship supported by key similarities.

Sometimes secondary differences cause conflict. But by appreciating each other's dissimilarities, spouses can grow by dealing successfully with the resulting challenges that may arise. So how do couples who are compatible in significant ways manage to stay happy together when faced with a difference that can be frustrating?

## Managing Irreconcilable Differences

In his extensive research, Psychologist John Gottman found that 69 percent of marriages' problems do not get *solved*.[5] But in good marriages, many problems are *managed*. Gottman states that couples can live with unresolvable conflicts about perpetual issues in their relationship if their differences are not deal breakers. It's not the presence of conflict that stresses the relationship; it's how the couple responds. Coping with differences positively and respectfully can keep a marriage thriving.

Couples who stay together happily learn to *manage* their differences. Sometimes it's as simple as agreeing to disagree, such as when spouses support different candidates for elected office or favor different political parties. In other situations, it's about finding a way to manage a difference. Couples who are willing to put their relationship first are likely to reach a successful resolution. The key is to be aware of, accept, and respect differences that need not be deal breakers.

## Caroline and Kyle Manage Differences

Caroline and Kyle are compatible in important ways. They share the same religious background, educational level, and significant values. They both like living in their quiet town in upstate New York. One big difference was that Kyle didn't want to become a parent, and Caroline longed for a baby. Kyle loved Caroline and put their relationship first. He decided to go along with her wish. He explained his decision philosophically by saying, "If you have children, or if you don't, you will regret it." It turned out that they both found parenting fulfilling. Now their son is married, and they adore their young grandchildren.

Kyle and Caroline have a security seeker/adventure seeker difference. He likes staying close to home, and she loves to travel. They manage this difference well. Caroline doesn't try to convince Kyle to act against his homebody nature, which would cause him to resent her for pressuring him. He doesn't try to force her into his stay-home mold by insisting that she stop taking trips.

Their solution: Caroline travels with women friends who share her interest in visiting places like Argentina, Denmark,

New Zealand, and elsewhere. Kyle misses her when she's gone but is glad to have a happy wife. Kyle and Caroline manage this difference—not by trying to change each other, but by accepting it and creating a solution that fits both of them.

## Some Differences Cannot Be Negotiated

Not all opposites or differences can be managed. Some potential deal breakers are

- different religions;
- different spending styles (e.g., one is frugal; the other spends wildly);
- different opinions on having children;
- different mental or physical conditions;
- different lifestyles (e.g., one wants to live in an urban area, the other in a rural one);
- different core values (e.g., one wants fame and fortune; the other wants a quiet, contemplative life); and
- different ideas about fidelity (e.g., open marriage versus traditional marriage).

## Enough Commonalities Are Important

Spouses with similar values, enough compatible interests, and good character traits are more likely to have lasting, fulfilling marriages. When differences arise in a good relationship, instead of judging their partner as "wrong," couples listen to each other and express themselves respectfully. They put their relationship first and find solutions that work for both of them.

# P is for

○ Patience
○ Pattern
○ Plan
○ Prayer
○ Preconceptions

## PATIENCE

A relaxed attitude is attractive; a desperate one is not. Trusting that you will marry the right person at the right time is a helpful outlook for your peace of mind and will make you more attractive to a prospective spouse.

You have all the time in the world. Okay, not exactly, but you're likely to succeed sooner by staying relaxed during your journey. So let the process unfold. Be patient with yourself and with people you meet and date. Trust your insides. You'll know when it's time to end a situation that's not good, and you'll sense when you're ready to move a relationship forward. Meanwhile, enjoy your time while single. Fill your life with pleasurable and meaningful experiences.

# PATTERN

If you've wanted to marry for a long time but it's not happening, there's a good chance that you've been getting in your way. To find out if you have a self-defeating pattern or if circumstances are holding you back, here are a few ideas:

- Ask a close friend or two who may have noticed how you act in social and dating situations. Does she see a pattern you should know about?
- Answer these questions on your own: Have you ended relationships when you sensed the man wanted to commit? Have you stayed too long in relationships with men who weren't interested in marriage?
- Ask yourself, "Am I avoiding opportunities for meeting or dating a potential marriage partner?"
- Ask yourself, "Have I recently experienced a significant life change that requires time to process or adjust to so that I simply don't have the energy to reach out and be receptive to others?" Examples of changes that can feel overwhelming are the passing of a family member or close friend, a divorce, job loss, or sudden financial reversal.

If your answer is yes to the first three of the above bulleted questions, you're probably in a self-defeating pattern, like Nancy, whose story appears below. But if circumstances beyond your control caused you to answer yes to the last question, then like Stephanie, whose story also is below, you're not necessarily experiencing a negative pattern.

## Nancy's Pattern

Nancy yearned to marry. She met men easily and often. She liked the excitement of having a new man in her life and not knowing how long he'd stick around. But if a man showed signs of becoming serious, Nancy would find him dull. She pined after men who wanted only a casual relationship. She stayed involved with them too long, fantasizing that they'd eventually marry her.

After Nancy complained to her friend Miriam about still another man who didn't want a serious relationship, Miriam said, "You're ambivalent. Part of you wants marriage, and part of you doesn't. You should get therapy." Nancy was taken aback by her friend's bluntness. She wasn't ready for the truth.

Subconsciously, Nancy feared a husband would abandon her. That happened to her mother when Nancy's father divorced her to marry another woman. Nancy acted out both her wish to marry and her fear of a heartbreaking divorce by continuing her self-defeating dating pattern for a long time. Eventually, Nancy recognized her pattern and received psychotherapy. Miriam was a bridesmaid at her wedding.

## Avoiding Opportunities: Alice and Patti

Alice, fifty-six, says she wants marriage but takes no initiative to meet men. She's been divorced twice. She secretly believes that if she tries again, it won't work out. Both she and her friend Patti play the "yes, but" game. When friends suggest ways to meet men, they reject their advice. They might respond to the idea of trying online dating by saying, "Yes, but I wouldn't do it; I've heard too many sad stories from people who tried it."

Patti, forty-six, won't go to singles events or use a matchmaking service because "the men all want someone younger, thinner, richer, or prettier."

Alice and Patti have similar patterns: they complain to their women friends about how hard it is to meet a good man, but they ignore opportunities to meet men and date.

## Sometimes It's Circumstances: Stephanie's Situation

A year after Stephanie's painful divorce, her mother died in a car accident. Her need to grieve both losses consumed nearly all her energy. She could barely work and was holding onto her job by a thread.

Stephanie wasn't involved in a pattern. She responded to her life's circumstances: one devastating loss on top of another, combined with the need to carry on and earn a living. Just before her mother's accident, Stephanie thought it might be time to start meeting men. Now the only new person in her life is her grief counselor. She needs time to heal, after which she'll probably start dating.

## Reversing an Unproductive Pattern

Here are ideas for reversing a pattern that may be preventing you from marrying:

- Get psychotherapy to help resolve your internal conflict.
- Attend singles events with a friend expecting that the two of you will enjoy yourselves.
- Talk informally with married friends who may serve as role models and educators for how to create a fulfilling, lasting union.
- Be open to meeting a potential marriage partner anywhere.

### *Exercise: Recognizing a Pattern*

By answering these questions, you may be able to recognize a self-defeating pattern:

1. Do you get high from the excitement of meeting someone new?
2. Do you find marriage-minded men boring or somehow inadequate?
3. Do you imagine that someone who doesn't want marriage will change his mind?

4. Do you recognize a conflict within yourself about marriage, similar to Nancy's?
5. If you are aware of such a conflict, what steps are you willing to take to resolve it?

# PLAN

*If you don't know where you're going,*
*you'll end up someplace else.*
—YOGI BERRA

"Follow your heart" sounds lovely. Your emotions are important. But if you want a successful marriage, basing your decisions mainly on your feelings is risky.

Research shows that to become happily married, we should plan thoughtfully. According to a study, "couples who are decisive before marriage — intentionally defining their relationships . . . appear to have better marriages than couples who simply let inertia carry them through major transitions."[1]

Early screening to learn if someone is marriage minded prevents misunderstandings. Yet many couples drift along rather than hold a conversation that defines their relationship. Instead, they slide into decisions, whether about sex, cohabitation, or even marriage, with unspoken expectations. Scott Stanley, a research professor at the University of Denver who co-authored the study mentioned above, states, "Relationships today are much more ambiguous. . . . If you define things, you risk breaking up."

If you are afraid to have "the talk," be brave. You'll benefit from learning whether it's worth investing your time and energy in the relationship.

If you want marriage, why stay involved with someone who wants companionship, sex, or fun, but not commitment? Let your intuition guide you about when to ask whether you're dating for the same purpose. Or, as you'll see below, a man might broach the subject.

## George Gets Right to the Point

Belinda didn't need to initiate the conversation because George did on their first date. This might be too soon for many, but it was okay for them. George said he wanted to get married and wouldn't continue dating anyone who didn't have the same goal. Belinda reassured him. After getting to know each other over time, George and Belinda married. They have three children and recently celebrated their twentieth anniversary.

## Are You Ready for Marriage?

Similarly, Larry, a handsome, kind social worker, said over lunch on our first date over thirty-five years ago, "I'm ready to settle down."

Suddenly, he stopped looking so attractive to me. Unlike Belinda, I wasn't yet ready for marriage. I wanted it but feared it wouldn't work out well. So once I sensed that a man wanted a serious relationship, I'd bolt. This was my pattern.

Larry probably sensed my unease. He didn't ask me out again.

But I did something good for him. I invited Larry to a party at my place, where he met Barbara. They've been happily married for thirty-four years.

## Implementing My Plan

I was in therapy to get past my conflict when I met my future husband. On our third date, I felt comfortable enough to ask David casually, "Are you hoping to marry and have children?" My tone conveyed no pressure, just curiosity. He said he wanted both. So I gathered we had compatible life goals and continued to see him.

The three scenarios above are examples of the first "talk," an initial screening to see if someone is marriage minded. Of course, you are not speaking about the two of you marrying. Most likely, you barely know each other. You're simply learning whether to continue dating this person.

Two of the above examples are of a man saying on a first date that he's looking to marry. Maybe a woman should wait longer to bring up the topic. Men generally want to feel like the pursuer, so a man might feel put on the spot if a woman tries to find out if he's marriage minded before they go out together at least a few times.

If he is marriage minded and you like him, you'll find out if he's the one in time.

If he signals that he doesn't want commitment, you might feel tempted to keep seeing him, hoping he'll change his mind. Don't count on that. If he caves in because you've pressured him, he may resent you long after tying the knot.

Your time is too precious to spend on someone who's not interested in marrying.

# PRAYER

Many people find that praying lightens a load that can feel too heavy to carry alone. They ask for help to overcome challenges.

If you're wondering how to pray, there's no formula. Speak from your heart. You can say how you feel and ask for what you want. You might request strength, perseverance, or wisdom to help you reach your goal.

Prayer can also be saying thank you, expressing gratitude for the blessings and miracles you experience.

# PRECONCEPTIONS

If you have a fixed idea about a trait you think you need in a husband, but it's minor in the grand scheme of things, consider broadening your horizons.

Aline expected to marry someone of average height with a full head of hair who was ambitious, like her high school boyfriend.

After eight years with him, she was happy to become engaged to him. But as the wedding date neared, he said it was over because he was in love with a coworker. Aline was devastated.

Then she met Brett, a lovely man who was, in her words, "not my type because he came in a different package from what I had in mind." He was short, starting to go bald, and not ambitious. He was kind, nonjudgmental, and could make her laugh, so she liked spending time with him while she wasn't ready for a serious relationship. That changed over time. Aline and Brett have now been happily married for twenty years.

The moral of Aline's story: let go of preconceived notions that can interfere with your long-term happiness. If you think he must be an Ivy League college graduate, have a particular occupation, ski, play tennis, or possess a specific physical characteristic, think again. Someone very different might turn out to be just right for you.

## Exercise

1. What qualities are you looking for in a husband that may be superficial?
2. What qualities may be more necessary for your long-term happiness than any other ones you've been thinking are essential?

 **is for**

○ **Qualify**
○ **Quirks**

## QUALIFY

When dating, do you qualify a prospective marriage partner to decide whether to keep seeing him? Salespeople qualify potential buyers. If you want a free vacation in exchange for listening to a sales pitch for a timeshare or something else, you'll first need to answer questions about your income, age, and so on. Sellers don't want to invest precious time on an unlikely prospect, and neither should you.

As your relationship continues, do an occasional reality check to make sure the two of you are on the same track. Ask qualifying questions as needed while being sensitive to the timing until the two of you have either gone your separate ways or closed the deal, i.e., set a wedding date.

## QUIRKS

All of us have quirks. So you might as well accept that whoever you marry will have a peculiarity or two.

Here are a few quirks that might bother you before or after marrying:

- He often says, "you know" or "uh" in the middle of a sentence.
- He sometimes chews with his mouth open.
- He leaves the seat up.
- He puts the toilet paper on its roller the "wrong" way.
- He snores.
- He rarely buys you flowers.

Yes, you can try to change him (good luck!), and sometimes you might succeed. But, assuming that what annoys you is too minor in the grand scheme of things to be a deal breaker, you'll be wise to learn to accept and ignore most things you cannot change. If you've asked him repeatedly, but to no avail, to eliminate "you knows" or the "uhs," you'll be happier if you learn to ignore the extraneous noises.

Also, you can work around quirks that bother you. You can buy the flowers yourself, possibly use separate bathrooms, and tell him to look in the mirror while he eats, but there will always be something.

You might ask yourself: "Am I so perfect?" He might notice a few of your quirks. Remember Estelle Reiner's advice: "Marry someone who can stand you."

The best way to deal with his quirks that you can live with, besides knowing that you too have foibles, is to keep noticing and telling him about his positive traits that you love and admire. You can expect him to reciprocate in kind.

# R is for

- References
- Religion
- Requests
- Resilience
- Respect
- Romance

## REFERENCES

Does it seem odd to get references for a possible dating partner or potential husband? With the popularity of online dating sites, it's smart to be careful before meeting a near stranger in person.

Arranged marriages, which are still the norm in some cultures, often result in happy unions when those who plan the match have each person's best interests in mind. The potential partners have been vetted by people who know them well, typically their parents or other family members. They're likely to have similar core values and realistic expectations for marriage.

If, as Natalie did, you meet your husband through someone who knows you well, you have a built-in reference. Sylvia told her friend Joan that her son, Jeffrey, wanted to meet a potential marriage partner. Joan had another friend, whose lovely daughter, Natalie, was also marriage minded. Jeffrey and Natalie began dating. They've now been happily married for over forty years.

But if you meet differently, getting references formally or informally at some point makes sense.

Gina and Milt, mentioned in Online Dating (page 116), had each met people who lied about themselves on the internet. So both agreed to give each other names and phone numbers of people who knew them well. Before meeting in person, each contacted the other's references and received glowing reports—a green light for their relationship to proceed. It evolved into a happy marriage and four children.

### References May Come Easily

My husband, David, and I first met at a singles event at a synagogue. After a few dates, he invited me to join his parents and aunt for Thanksgiving dinner. I felt comfortable with his family. Several months later, a mutual acquaintance said, "David is one of the sincerest and smartest people I know." We were already engaged by then, yet I felt buoyed by her endorsement.

### Making It Safe

Even with references, if you decide to meet someone in person who began as an internet acquaintance, choose a public and populated venue, like a coffee shop rather than your home. Some women still balk at the idea of meeting someone online, but many others have done so and are now in good marriages.

If you're in the same social circle and get to know him over time and meet his friends and see how they get along, that's ideal. But if this isn't your experience, seek references casually or formally.

# RELIGION

Faith means different things to different people. According to many, faith is the belief that G-d exists.[1] Most Americans say they believe in G-d, which they may understand differently, perhaps

136 | Marriage Minded

as a positive transcendent force, higher power, or universe that wants to help.[2]

If you have faith, meaning that you trust things to work out well, you'll find it easier to relax and enjoy dating. If one man turns out not to be right for you, this will mean that you are one closer to finding the one who is.

Without trusting that you deserve and can create a good marriage, it's easy to get discouraged. You might give up and create a busy social life with friends or stay in a going-nowhere relationship because you don't think you can do better.

"I'm not religious, but I'm spiritual," some people say. (See Spirituality, page 161.) Whatever you call your belief system, which may include a supernatural element, you'll shine with confidence by integrating its wisdom into your daily life. You'll trust that you'll meet the right man at the right time and create a fulfilling marriage.

It's normal to have doubts about the existence of something our five senses cannot perceive. You can strengthen your faith by spending time with people you respect, who strive to live according to their spiritual or religious ideals.

Your religion or spirituality is part of your identity. Not everyone recognizes its importance. If yours is or may become important to you, date people who fit with your belief system and your core identity. Don't lie to yourself by saying, "Religion doesn't matter." It does matter.

# REQUESTS

In a good relationship, partners express appreciation often. They also say gently what they want and what they don't want. Neither one expects the other to read her or his mind.

So don't be afraid to ask for what you want.

Keeping a grievance inside can cause a grudge to build. By calmly bringing up what's bothering you or saying what you desire, you're likely to clear the air and renew warm feelings.

This doesn't mean we should point out every minor fault in the other or be overly demanding. For a relationship to stay healthy, it's important to tolerate minor annoyances and to focus on how the two of you get along overall.

No one wants to feel criticized. Process your thoughts and emotions before speaking up. Instead of holding on to feeling wronged, you'll be able to focus more on what you'd like the person to do differently. Your words, voice tone, and body language can show loving concern.

## Examples of How to Request

Lynne liked Hunter very much. The first time he flirted with a waitress, she thought she might be imagining it. She didn't want to make a big deal over what could be nothing, so she didn't say anything. But it happened two more times. She felt insecure. He was thirty-five and said he was ready to settle down, but he wasn't acting that way. Lynne thought he couldn't be serious about her if he enjoyed chatting up waitresses. She was tempted to stop seeing him, but not yet because he had so many good qualities.

Finally, she told Hunter, "I like being with you very much. I think you'd want me to tell you about something that's bothering me. When you flirt with waitresses, I'm uncomfortable. I want to feel special to you like I'm the only woman you find attractive."

Hunter took her message to heart. He said, "It's a bad habit. I'm sorry I made you uncomfortable. It's my insecurity showing. I think I wanted you to be jealous, to prove women like me. I won't do it again."

Had she withheld her feelings and her request, Lynne probably would have developed a grudge and ended the relationship. Instead, she gave him a gift: the opportunity to correct his behavior.

Maybe you'd be annoyed by someone who regularly interrupts you, is often late, or forgets your birthday. For whatever you need to address, it calls for a respectful conversation that focuses on what you'd like him to do differently.

## Accepting Requests Graciously

In a good relationship, requests go both ways. Consider, for example, that he dislikes being interrupted by you, that it makes him lose his train of thought. You may instantly feel offended. But if he's telling the truth respectfully, thank him, even if he doesn't say what he wants instead, such as, "I'd like you to be patient, so I can finish speaking before you respond."

Constructive feedback offered compassionately helps us grow. When we become aware of how our behavior upsets someone, we'll be able to shift gears and do better. We'll probably also improve our relationships with friends, family members, and others.

## Polishing the Rough Edges

Partners in a good relationship focus on each other's positive qualities. They respond to each other's imperfections graciously and constructively.

Reproach is like sandpaper. Couples who use it wisely, by nicely saying what they would like to be different, smooth out each other's rough edges over time while remaining emotionally close.

Jen explains how she does this with her husband. He leaves crumbs on the counter, which annoys her. She tells him pleasantly, "It would help me out if you would wipe the crumbs off the counter."

Another woman, Connie, knew how to ask for what she desired. Her fiancé, a former hippie, thought engagement rings were a frivolous expense. Instead of fretting over his lack of generosity, Connie showed him a sapphire ring in a jewelry store's window and said sweetly, "It would make me very happy if you'd give me this one." Married for over thirty years, she still wears the ring.

However, regardless of how pleasantly you ask, there's no guarantee that the person will do what you want. But how will you know if you don't try? Regardless of the outcome, you're likely to learn something. You may learn to accept minor imperfections or that the world doesn't come to an end when we ask for what we want. Or, as often happens, we learn that our partner wants to please us and to do his best to make us happy.

# RESILIENCE

*The course of true love never did run smooth.*
—WILLIAM SHAKESPEARE

Disappointments are likely to occur during your journey toward marriage. View them as bumps in the road from which you can bounce back and learn.

We can increase resilience by

- planning for how we want to conduct ourselves in a relationship;
- staying objective while dating; and
- grieving a past relationship, if necessary, to gain closure.

By doing what's needed to keep going forward, you're likely to move more quickly toward a successful marriage.

## Planning for a New Relationship

Suppose you've found in the past that becoming physically or emotionally involved with someone too soon causes you to crash into a depression when the relationship ends. Your sadness is likely to have prevented you from entering a new healthy relationship.

So you might consider a different way of dating, perhaps by being warm and friendly while signaling a lack of readiness for sexual involvement.

## Staying Objective While Dating

On a similar note, you can plan to stay objective about a relationship partner by staying aware of your feelings while keeping your brain in charge. In other words, say no to instant infatuation and yes to moving beyond fantasy. Notice how compatible the two of you are over time. Do you have shared values and goals? Do you have enough in common in other ways for a lasting, happy marriage?

## Grieving to Gain Closure about a Past Relationship

This may sound paradoxical, but sometimes we need to go backward to move forward toward a goal. Lingering feelings about a relationship that ended unhappily can keep us stuck in sadness. By grieving enough to process emotions and learn from the experience, we gain energy to bring our best selves into a new relationship. You can read more about grieving on page 48.

Grieving in any way that fits you will help you recover more quickly from a relationship that ended badly and restore you sooner to your terrific self.

# RESPECT

Is *respectful* on your list of ten traits you want in a spouse?

One of the "four horsemen" that destroy marriage, states marriage researcher and psychologist John Gottman, is contemptuous behavior, often demonstrated by rolling eyes or putting down one's partner in front of other people. The other horsemen are criticism, defensiveness, and stonewalling.[3] These behaviors show a lack of respect, with the possible exception of occasional defensiveness, because who's perfect?

A respectful person will give you his full attention when you are speaking. He'll listen courteously. He may validate your feelings and thoughts when you share them. He'll encourage you to say what's on your mind. He will guard your honor as though it were his own, meaning he'll be polite to you when others are present.

Of course, we should give the other person the same kind of regard that we expect to receive. Mutual respect is vital for a healthy relationship.

Self-respect is essential too. We respect ourselves by holding to our boundaries. (For more about this, see Boundaries, page 15.) We also show respect for others by accepting their boundaries.

# ROMANCE

Fairy tales and romantic novels glorify romance. But how does this apply to real life? Romance is lovely, but for passion, ardor, and desire to last, a couple needs to have enough similar fundamental values, interests, lifestyle preferences, and worthy character traits.

## Keeping a Clear Head

Suppose you meet a charming man, and before you know it, you're fantasizing about happily ever after. You imagine a future before you know whether he will be honest, trustworthy, and kind in the long run. If this sounds familiar, stop!

Sociopaths can be charming and exciting. Narcissists too, until you get to know them better. So do stay objective while seeing how the person behaves in everyday life and how he relates to you over time.

While some marriages based on "love at first sight" turn out well, most do not.

Suppose you go out with someone a couple of times. You have enough in common and enjoy each other's company. Let your relationship progress at a comfortable pace. Get to know each other gradually.

It's natural for people to feel nervous about making a good impression at first, so don't expect chemistry right away. If you feel no connection after a reasonable time, maybe three or four dates, it may be time to move on.

## Giving Romance a Chance

Sometimes people start as friends and eventually become involved romantically. After Mindy had known Jack as a friend for quite a while, she offered to introduce him to a woman she thought he might want to date. Jack looked surprised. "What about you and me?" he asked.

Mindy had no idea he'd been thinking of her that way. They started dating, and she developed romantic feelings for him. Now, good friends and lovers, she and Jack have been happily married for twenty years and have two children.

# S is for

- Secrets
- Self-Awareness
- Self-Esteem
- Self-Nurture
- Self-Talk
- Serendipity
- Sex: Different Ways for Different Women
- Sex: What Research Reveals
- Space
- Spirituality
- Spontaneity

## SECRETS

Who doesn't have a secret that might feel embarrassing to share? It makes sense to be open with a potential life partner about anything that might be a deal breaker. This doesn't mean engaging in a free-for-all of venting about past relationships or other sensitive matters before you know him well. It means understanding that there is a time to conceal and another time to reveal anything that might seriously affect your relationship.

### Mimi's Secret

Mimi, forty-one, an attractive, successful marketing professional, had a secret. It had been over ten years since she'd been hospitalized for bipolar disorder. Once she started taking the prescribed medicine, she continued to function well. Yet she still felt vulnerable, unsure if her problems were over. She felt ashamed of her past bizarre behaviors. Some of her friends had become distant. She understood that many people fear what they don't understand, but it still hurt.

Now that she was seriously dating Dustin, she would need to tell him at some point before marrying him if their relationship progressed that way. But when?

My advice to Mimi applies to any secret that you wouldn't want to broadcast on social media or the seven o'clock news: "Only when you're close to becoming engaged should you disclose a possible deal-breaking secret."

You're bigger than your secret. If you expose it too soon, you risk being typecast as defective. First, let him know you as the lovely, talented, multifaceted person you are. Once he's ready to commit, assuming you've chosen well, he's likely to value you as much as ever, and perhaps more, for trusting him with your secret.

Just about everyone has a secret. Perhaps one or both of you grew up in a dysfunctional family whose issues continue to affect you, which is true for many of us to some degree. Other secrets, which are more common than you might think, include having been the victim of verbal, sexual, or physical abuse or having a mental or physical illness.

Possibly, he has a secret that might be a deal breaker for you. When a proposal seems likely, you may want to ask him something like, "Is there anything I should know about you that might affect our relationship in the future?"

After Mimi realized that Dustin was going to propose, she said she needed to share something personal with him in case it made a difference. She told him about her psychiatric history. He was surprised. After thinking it over, he proposed a week later. They've now been happily married for over twenty-five years, and Mimi's mental health has been fine.

*Exercise*

Answering these questions can guide you to deal with your secret(s) while dating or after marrying. Explain your answers.

1. Do you agree with Mimi's decision to wait so long to reveal her secret to Dustin? If not, what would you have done instead?
2. What private information do you think calls for discretion? How will you decide whether and when to reveal it to a romantic partner?
3. What kinds of secrets are best to keep to yourself even after marrying? You can gain support regarding a secret by sharing it with someone other than a romantic partner.
4. In whom do you feel comfortable confiding who is not a romantic partner? He or she might be a friend, family member, therapist, counselor, or someone else.
5. Are you okay with having a romantic partner who keeps certain secrets from you?

# SELF-AWARENESS

Self-awareness keeps us on track in relationships. People who understand themselves will naturally be more desirable marriage partners. Because they accept the whole package of who they are, they are likely to be accepting of and empathic toward themselves and others. A key to creating a fulfilling, lasting marriage is to know and accept your true self.

**To increase self-awareness, know**
- *who you really are.*

What are your strengths, weaknesses, likes, and dislikes? Self-acceptance is crucial during any stage of a lifelong journey of self-discovery. We are all works in progress and can grow in whatever direction we choose. In the meantime, love yourself.

Enjoy being who you are; your whole combination and your glow will attract men who also have healthy self-esteem.

- *how you feel.*

If we want intimacy, we need to be aware of our emotions. Sharing them can make us feel vulnerable. If we grew up in a family that discouraged expressing feelings or labeled them as right or wrong, we might be afraid to reveal our true selves as adults. But emotional intimacy requires self-expression. Sharing one's authentic self with a partner must happen to create an emotionally and spiritually fulfilling marriage.

- *what you can contribute to the relationship.*

Which traits of yours will your future husband probably value? By recognizing your good qualities, you'll come across as confident and are likely to attract a man who has a positive self-image. To acknowledge your attractive attributes, see Lists, page 79. Appealing qualities include intelligence, kindness, a sense of humor, resourcefulness, empathy, creativity, generosity, humility, and others.

Showing humility doesn't mean denying the existence of your excellent attributes; it means recognizing them as gifts for which you're grateful, not boastful. Humility also means realizing that we all have imperfections and room to grow, as noted in Humility, page 58.

# SELF-ESTEEM

True self-esteem fosters an optimistic attitude, good dating relationships, and a great marriage.

If you sense that you lack self-esteem, you can develop it. Religious and spiritual approaches, psychotherapy, and other activities can contribute to gaining, regaining, or maintaining our self-esteem during life's ups and downs. Most belief systems affirm that we're all here for a reason and that each of us is capable of accomplishing the mission we were put on earth to do.

# SELF-NURTURE

Meeting new people and dating take energy. It's easy to feel depleted over time while seeking a husband. If you haven't found anyone suitable, or if you thought you did but it didn't work out, you may feel tempted to give up.

## Energy in, Energy out

You can prevent burnout by recharging your battery regularly. An excellent way to do this is to date yourself! As noted earlier, in *The Artist's Way,* Julia Cameron writes that all of us should go out alone on a weekly date. Doing so allows us to escape life's pressures, tune into our uncensored thoughts and feelings, and keep our creative juices flowing.

Making a date with yourself means avoiding the temptation to include a friend. Do things on your own that keep you feeling vital and happy. You might enjoy a solitary walk in the woods, taking yourself out for tea or dinner on your own, swimming, meditating or praying, journaling, receiving a massage, taking a hot bath, reading in a peaceful place without distractions, or something else.

Dates with yourself revive you as a unique individual who naturally radiates the kind of aliveness that attracts suitable men like a magnet.

Maybe you feel refreshed after getting together with a friend. That's fine too, but doing this doesn't replace a weekly date with just yourself. We connect to our essence by doing pleasurable activities on our own. We exude aliveness and desirability.

Some women become so focused on meeting and dating men that they forget to date themselves. In case you need ideas for dates with yourself and uplifting activities to do with others,

*Taking time for self-nurture.*

you can create your list of possibilities by doing the chart exercise shown in the Joy entry on page 73.

# SELF-TALK

Did you know that the most important person to communicate with is yourself? Using self-talk effectively can save a relationship.

*Self-talk* refers to the messages we give ourselves. We can use the self-talk technique to change unhelpful inner speech into positive, supportive communication. Here's the five-step method to do this, provided by psychologist Pamela Butler, author of *Talking to Yourself: How Cognitive Behavior Therapy Can Change Your Life:*

**Step 1.** *Be aware.* Listen to your own self-talk. What are you telling yourself?

**Step 2.** *Evaluate.* Decide if your inner dialogue is supportive or destructive.

**Step 3.** *Identify.* Determine the source of the thinking error that is maintaining your inner speech. Is it

- the Driver, an inner self who commands you to be perfect, hurry up, be strong, please others, or try hard;
- the Stopper, an inner self who catastrophizes, self-labels, self-judges in harmful ways, and sets rigid requirements; or
- the Confuser, an inner self who makes arbitrary inferences, fails to be aware of the full picture, overgeneralizes, and makes other cognitive distortions?

**Step 4.** *Support yourself.* Replace your negative self-talk with permission and self-affirmation. For example, if you are inclined to please others too often at your own expense, you can replace negative self-talk with permission to satisfy yourself. You can tell yourself:

"At times, it is important for me to do or say what I want, even if my doing so does not please the other person at the moment."

Step 5. *Develop your guide.* Decide what action you need to take based on your new supportive position.

## Carla's Self-Talk Saves Her Relationship

Carla had been dating Russell for a couple of months, so she felt confused when he told her on the phone that he'd be celebrating his birthday with close family members. It was too soon to know where the relationship would be going, but all seemed well until this happened. Here's how Carla used the self-talk technique to prevent herself from sabotaging their relationship:

*What about me?* she thought, feeling her stomach tighten when the call ended. *If Russell cared for me, he'd want to be with me on his birthday.* Here's how Carla recognized and reversed her negative self-talk, using the above five-step process:

1. *Be aware.* "I'm telling myself he doesn't like me, that he's not taking me seriously."
2. *Evaluate.* "My self-talk is unhelpful; it makes me feel bad about both Russell and myself."
3. *Identify.* "The source of my thinking error is my *Confuser*. It's causing me to make an arbitrary inference, i.e., illogical conclusion. I'm not seeing the whole picture."
4. *Support yourself.* "I'm giving myself permission to ask Russell why he's not including me in his birthday plan."
5. *Develop your guide.* Carla's action plan: Keep an open mind. Carla decides to phone Russell and say, gently, "I'm surprised that you don't want to celebrate your birthday with me," and see what happens.

Can you see how Carla has used self-talk to get out of her funk? Are you wondering how Russell responded to her comment?

Actually, Russell had wanted to be with Carla for his birthday, but because she hadn't invited him to dinner or suggested something else for his special day, he thought it wasn't important to her. So he'd gone along with his parents' idea for a family dinner at a restaurant. "Would you like to join us?" he asked Carla.

What if Carla hadn't reversed her negative self-talk? She might have sulked, harbored hurt feelings, and stopped seeing Russell. Fortunately, Carla's positive self-talk resulted in a happy ending. And a year later, a happy marriage.

But really, any outcome from positive self-talk is likely to be constructive. What if Russell had implied that he wasn't that interested in her? Carla would have been disappointed but ultimately relieved to free herself from a going-nowhere relationship and find a better one.

One way or another, using the self-talk communication technique is likely to produce calmness, objectivity, and a satisfying sense of closure.

# SERENDIPITY

Serendipity is "the faculty or phenomenon of finding valuable or agreeable things not sought for."[1] Amazing things can result from appreciating unexpected occurrences that just seem to happen.

Aline, whose story appears earlier (in Preconceptions, page 130), tells how her acceptance of the unexpected allowed her to continue dating Brett. He was quite different from the kind of man she thought was right for her. She expected to marry someone like her ex-fiancé, who was of average height, had a full head of hair, and maintained a high-status career. She was devastated after he broke off their engagement.

Then she met Brett, who was short, "showed up without much hair," and had a low-key job he disliked. Because she wasn't ready for anything serious, she spent time with him, expecting nothing.

Aline eventually realized that the packaging was less important than what was inside. She married Brett. But had she not been open to serendipity, he would have stayed beneath her radar. Instead, Aline got to know him. She was impressed by his kindness, integrity, sense of humor, and joie de vivre. She realized in time that such traits are more important than more superficial ones.

Whether you call it serendipity, fate, Divine Providence, or something else,[2] be ready to accept and welcome someone into your life whose appearance, age, occupation, or other feature differs from what you had in mind. He just might be right for you. And he can show up anytime.

# SEX: DIFFERENT WAYS FOR DIFFERENT WOMEN

In the old days, girls learned that sex was for marriage. Today, guidelines are often less clear. When or whether to become sexually involved is usually a personal choice. Here's how several women explain their decision:

- **Gwen:** "I had sex almost right away with Joseph. Only after marriage did I realize that we were very different in our values and interests. Sex was the only good thing in our marriage, and it stayed great until we divorced. It's important to take a 'test drive' so you'll know if your bodies fit well and if you like his smell."
- **Janet:** "If you can't tell the difference between sex and love, don't have sex. I sometimes used to have sex with someone I was dating. But I'd think it was love and be miserable when it didn't work out. So I decided to start acting like a virgin. After getting engaged to a wonderful man when I was thirty-one, I stopped being a virgin. We've been married for thirty-three years."
- **Laura:** "You can have good sex before marriage like we did, but things can change after. The stresses of earning a living

and raising children caused my child's father to disengage from me sexually. We ended up divorcing."

- **Rona:** "My husband and I started dating in high school and knew we wanted to marry. We had sex before marrying five years later. We had a wonderful marriage for fifty years until he passed away."
- **Lorraine:** "I was done with the emotional turmoil I used to get after being in casual relationships that became sexual. I told myself: *No more sex without commitment*. I needed to know we were *definitely* getting married. So I waited until our wedding night. Matt was understanding. Thirty years later, we still have good sex."
- **Mitzi:** "Aaron and I were both in our mid-seventies when we started dating, sometime after his wife had passed away. I'd known him when he was married and saw what a kind and loyal husband he'd been. He moved into my place about a year before we got married eight years ago. Aaron is a wonderful husband, thoughtful, and patient. These have been the best years of my life."

## Should You Take a Test Drive?

By thinking through your sexual boundaries in advance, you'll be more likely to make good decisions.

A test drive can go either way. Let's say the sex is fabulous. But if you don't know him too well, it could turn out to be the only good thing in your relationship. For most women, compartmentalization doesn't work so well in this area. If he lacks the essential qualities you need, he's likely to become less physically appealing to you over time.

Perhaps, on the other hand, you're dating someone with whom you're compatible. You have similar values, interests, and lifestyle preferences. He has outstanding character traits. Then you take a test drive and are disappointed. You might decide to stop seeing him. But if you're married, you won't give up so easily.

You'll try harder because you're committed. So you're more likely to communicate in ways that lead to sexual pleasure and excitement for both of you.

## Should You Have Sex in an Uncommitted Relationship?

Some marriage-minded women think there's no downside to having casual sex with a man who's not interested in marriage while they look elsewhere for a husband. But sex produces more oxytocin, the "love hormone," in women than in men. The surge of oxytocin may well cause you to feel emotionally attached. When this happens, your interest in finding a marriage-minded man will become half-hearted, and such men will sense this.

The "high" of sex in an uncommitted relationship is often based on fantasy. It's fueled by the kind of novelty and unpredictability of a roller-coaster ride. Lasting intimacy requires trust, and trust takes time. It means knowing your partner is there for you in good times and in other times—for life.

Ideally, sexual intimacy is a physical, emotional, and spiritual experience that reflects and enhances love, trust, and respect. A good marriage provides the foundation for this. In this type of union, spouses feel free to express the totality of their being, knowing their relationship is intended to be lifelong and that no one is going away.

## Sex by the Third Date?

Many women have heard that they must have sex by the third date or the guy will lose interest. But if you do it to keep a man around, that's desperation, not love, and he'll sense it.

If a man is mature and a good prospect for marriage, he's likely to be patient and not pressure you. He'll be more interested in creating a future with you than in his immediate gratification at your possible emotional expense.

## How Can You Tell If He's Marriage Minded?

If your goal is marriage and he's asking for sex, you're entitled to find out whether he's marriage minded. In a relaxed way, you can ask him whether he's looking for marriage or for something else. Assure him that you're not talking about him committing to anyone in particular; you're just wondering what his thoughts are in general.

This sort of direct approach can surprise a man who wants to stay single. But if he wants sex yet balks at the thought of commitment, shouldn't you know?

## Ellie's Story

When Henry signaled to Ellie on a date that he wanted sex, she asked him casually if he wanted to get married. "Sure," he said in a tone that implied "perhaps someday."

Barely missing a beat, Ellie said, "When?" Surprised, he sputtered something vague. He got the message, and their friendship stayed platonic. Ellie married someone else a year later. Henry came to the wedding.

## How to Say "I'm Not Ready"

If he wants sex and you like him but aren't ready, you can tell him so with words or nonverbally. If he's making moves, you can be subtle by moving away from him slightly while maintaining a friendly manner. Doing so can be much more useful than engaging in a lengthy, perhaps sexually stimulating or frustrating, discussion. Whether you tell him directly or indirectly, he should get the message. A good potential husband will respect your wishes.

## What Does a Test Drive Really Prove?

A test drive may confirm that the two of you are sexually fine together at the time. But if this happens before you know him well, the satisfying sex might blind you to some red flags that could become deal breakers.

One woman said her test drive went well. Then, after a couple of years of marriage, the man told her he was gay.

The most important sexual organ is between the ears.[3] How you relate outside the bedroom over time is the best predictor of the kind of sex life you'll have in the long run. Your decision about whether or when to have sex should depend on your physical and emotional readiness, values, comfort level, and common sense.

## Exercise

1. Do you think it's necessary to take a test drive for sexual compatibility early in a relationship? Explain your answer.
2. Do you think Gwen (page 152) would have kept seeing Joseph if she'd gotten to know him better over time instead of quickly making their relationship sexual?
3. Which of the above women's viewpoints rings true for you, and why?

# SEX: WHAT RESEARCH REVEALS

The authors of a study involving 2,035 married participants state that "sexual intimacy in the early stages of dating is sometimes viewed as an important part of testing compatibility, and determining whether a relationship would work later on." However, the study reveals that "the longer a couple waited to become sexually involved, the better that sexual quality, relationship communication, relationship satisfaction, and perceived relationship stability was in marriage."

The timing of sex for couples in the study ranged from before the first date to after marriage. The study found that the longer they waited, the greater the relationship satisfaction over time.[4]

Mark Regnerus, PhD, of the University of Texas, says the study suggests to him that couples who "prioritize sex promptly at the outset of a relationship often find their relationships underdeveloped when it comes to the qualities that make relationships stable and spouses reliable and trustworthy."[5]

## Arranged Marriages

Another study looked into arranged marriages, which are still common in India, Pakistan, and other cultures. Despite widespread skepticism about such unions (because those that don't work out well may not have considered the couple's compatibility as a priority), this research shows that "feelings of love in arranged marriages tend to gradually increase as time goes on . . . whereas in so-called 'love marriages,' where attraction is based on passionate emotions, a couple's feelings for each other typically diminish by as much as 50 percent after only eighteen to twenty-four months of marriage."[6]

According to a study conducted in India, "arranged marriages appear to surpass love marriages in intensity at the five-year mark and be twice as strong as love marriages within ten years."[7] These are not forced marriages. "The parents and the son or daughter make the decision together; everyone is interested in everyone else's benefit."[8] The couple gets to see if mutual attraction exists before agreeing to marry.

## Love at First Sight

The idea of strangers finding each other across a crowded room and instantly falling in love is alluring. I still get misty-eyed watching the musical *South Pacific,* when handsome Emile sings "Some Enchanted Evening" to adorable Nellie on a tropical beach. But research shows that early passion usually does not result in a successful, lasting marriage in real life.

## What about Cohabitating?

Although cohabitation has been consistently associated with increased risk for divorce and marital distress in the United States, living together as an unmarried couple has become common today.

However, a study suggests that couples who cohabit and make a thoughtful decision to do so with the intention of marrying are more likely to have lasting marriages than couples who live together for convenience or to save money. The latter type of couple tends to "slide" into marriage rather than to carefully think through what's involved.[9]

The chart below is a simple, rough sketch that suggests some short-term and long-term pros and cons of sex in an uncommitted relationship. The topic is more complicated than one that can be divided into four boxes. The chart below can be a starting point, or you can make your own list of short- and long-term pros and cons of sex without commitment.

## If You Want Marriage, Should You Have Sex Without Commitment?

**Short-term pros**
- It feels great, exciting, and it makes you glow.
- It makes you happy.
- It's romantic and makes you feel loved.

**Short-term cons**
- You might be blinded by oxytocin-induced bonding and mistakenly think he feels as emotionally involved with you as you do with him.
- When you find out that he's having sex with other women or he simply disappears from your life, it can feel emotionally devastating.

**Long-term pros**
- Many married couples who've had sex with each other before committing do have good marriages.
- Couples who plan to marry and live together first are more likely to stay married than those who live together for convenience and drift into marriage as the next logical step.[10]

**Long-term cons**
- Unconsciously, a woman who has bonded emotionally (via oxytocin) with a marriage-averse partner is likely to send out "I'm not available" signals to other men. Consequently, she's likely to prevent herself from attaining her goal of marrying.

## Exercise

If you are dating someone and wonder about having sex, answer these questions:

1. Is having sex with him likely to lead to the future commitment that you want?
2. How do you decide when and with whom to become involved sexually?

# SPACE

We all need some space to stay centered and in touch with our true selves. By forgetting to pay attention to yourself as a unique, separate being, it's easy to lose your grounding or sense of self when in a relationship. Staying aware of our feelings and needs can be challenging for many women while emotionally involved with a man.

## Julie Learns to Take Space for Herself

Julie found it easy to meet men. From the time she started dating as a teenager until her early forties, it was one relationship after another. After each painful breakup, she needed a long time to grieve, recover, and regain a sense of herself as a separate, worthwhile person.

What made it so hard for Julie to rebound? She became so consumed by each relationship that she would lose herself in it.

Value yourself as a unique person. Be aware of how you feel and what you need to stay centered, whether or not a man is in your life. Julie's challenge was to learn to balance the energy she put into a relationship with the energy she invested in herself. She especially needed to take enough space for self-nurturing activities to do on her own and for taking care of herself in other essential ways (see Self-Nurture, page 147, and Balance, page 9).

## Distance Is Required to Stay Objective

To view a person or situation objectively requires distance. If our minds and hearts become filled with images, thoughts, and romantic fantasies about someone, we can easily forget to notice whether this person is good for us.

Something clicked for Julie when she was in her early forties. She felt awkward doing this, but she tried something different with Hector, a new man in her life. She was crazy about him— crazy because this happens to women like Julie, who lose their minds by falling in love with someone they barely know.

## Julie Retreats to Nap

On their second date, Julie and Hector had just returned to her place after taking a walk together. They planned to go out to dinner. Julie's feelings for him were so intense that she felt stressed. She realized that she needed a break. She told Hector that she'd like to take a short nap in her bedroom before dinner, and he was welcome to relax in the living room while she rested. He looked a bit surprised but was accepting.

Julie's intense yearning to bond had been interfering with her need to get enough distance to evaluate a relationship objectively. She was more careful with Hector. After four dates, she realized he wasn't likely to commit, so she stopped seeing him.

This time Julie needed almost no recovery time because she'd been able to free herself from a going-nowhere relationship quickly.

## Happy Ending for Julie

Julie soon met Jonah. She liked his calm, thoughtful manner and felt like she could be herself with him. Although she was physically attracted to him and sensed he was marriage minded, Julie took her time getting to know him. Because she understood that physical intimacy without commitment wasn't emotionally healthy for her, she went slowly in this area. Jonah respected her boundaries and her need for space. After six months, he proposed marriage.

Julie and Jonah have now been happily married for twenty-five years. The romance continues, and so does their respect for their own and each other's needs for space.

Giving yourself enough separate space in whatever way works for you is the best way to stay tuned into you. Julie's short nap during a long date was her way of getting back to her center. In between dates with a man, you might restore your balance by scheduling enough dates with just yourself, such as relaxing at a beach, hiking, reading a novel, swimming, listening to or playing music, drawing, painting, doing yoga, or something else.

A powerful yearning to bond can make us forget to use common sense to evaluate a relationship. Like Julie learned to do, we all need to take breaks to reclaim ourselves.

# SPIRITUALITY

A friend recently said to me about an acquaintance of hers, "I think you'd like Ann. She was raised Catholic, but she's very spiritual."

*Spiritual*, I thought. *What the heck does that mean?* The word can mean just about anything. So if *spiritual* is on the list of qualities you want in your future spouse, think about what that word means to you.

## Religion and Spirituality

Perhaps because they view religion as limiting rather than life enhancing, some people differentiate between religion and spirituality. I think this is a false distinction. So-called religious people may or may not exude spirituality, and people who appear to be spiritual may or may not identify with an established religion.

## Definitions of Spirituality Differ

Here are some traits many view as spiritual:

- believing in a metaphysical reality that we cannot perceive via any of our five senses;
- having insights and epiphanies, making connections;
- seeing the best in others, treating them with kindness and respect;
- being supportive and understanding;
- being generous;
- connecting on a soul or essence level;
- living thoughtfully and according to one's religious or philosophical beliefs;
- loving animals and humans; and
- believing in peace and love.

When choosing a spouse wisely, if you want a spiritual person, you probably consider yourself one. So ask yourself what you mean by the word as it applies to yourself and how you hope it will be noticeable in your future spouse.

We are all spiritual beings, capable of experiencing "aha" moments in which we intuitively grasp a truth that we hadn't recognized earlier. We may feel called to enter a profession or just know with certainty that an action or person is right or wrong for us.

People we perceive as not so spiritual may act more impulsively or selfishly than is healthy for a relationship. Most of us probably think people who thoughtfully consider the consequences of their actions are spiritual.

If you want children, it's essential to seek an agreement before committing to marriage about in what, if any, religion or spiritual practice you'll raise them. This discussion can help you learn whether you and a potential life partner have similar core values.

## Exercise

The questions below are designed to help you clarify whether your religious or spiritual views are compatible with those of a potential life partner.

1. With what, if any, religion were you raised?
2. How does the belief system you may have internalized while growing up affect you now?
3. How important is it for you to marry someone whose religion and religious (or spiritual) practice is overall like yours?
4. How do you define *spirituality*?
5. How do you define *soul*?
6. How will your definitions of *spirituality* and *soul* influence your choice of a future spouse?
7. If you're hoping to have children, with what religion or spiritual practice do you want to raise them? When should you find out if you and a possible future spouse agree?

# SPONTANEITY

*Spontaneity* means abandon, ease, lightheartedness, and openness,[11] all of which can be appealing qualities. How do you become more spontaneous? Just by being *you*, even when this means acting differently from your usual self. Let's say you're usually a careful planning type. Lighten up sometimes. Decide on the spur of the moment to drive off for an adventure, alone or with someone. Who knows? Maybe one day you'll suddenly get on a plane . . .

# Committing

 **is for**

- ○ **Teamwork**
- ○ **Testing**
- ○ **Therapy**
- ○ **Trauma**
- ○ **Trust**

## TEAMWORK

Good teamwork promotes mutual contentment. Notice how the two of you cooperate and share responsibilities. Do you both volunteer to do parts of what's needed? Do you each usually follow through by doing what you've agreed to do without reminders?

Teamwork can take time to develop as you learn about each other's strengths and preferences. A typical arena for teamwork can be where one cooks and the other cleans up and washes dishes. Or one person might do all that, and the other does the shopping, yard work, or other chores. There's no rule for who does what. Each couple figures out what works best for the two of them.

# TESTING

Marriage is one of life's most meaningful events, perhaps its most significant one. If you hope to marry, how do you know whether he's right for you *and* he's ready to commit?

Chemistry matters. So do good character traits, similar values and goals, intellectual compatibility, and enough shared interests. You can do some litmus testing to learn which qualities in a marriage partner you can accept and which ones spell trouble.

## We Can't Force Readiness

Marriage readiness is necessary and can't be forced. When he's ready, he's ready and not a moment before. If you're able to manipulate a *not-ready person into* marrying you, he may resent you for a long time. So test for readiness.

The *Sex and the City* television characters once compared a marriage-ready man to a taxi: He becomes ready to commit at a certain time. His "available" light goes on, and the next woman in his life gets the ring. You can tell the difference between a man who's got the light on and one who's just driving around in the dark. Here are some positive signs of his readiness:

- The singles scene no longer appeals to him.
- He's at least able to talk about the idea of commitment.
- He wants to be a dad or is willing to be a stepdad.
- He's financially independent.
- He's your boyfriend in name—your husband in spirit. He makes plans for the future, introduces you to his family and friends. He checks in with you regularly, wants to hear about your day and tell you about his.
- He's open and honest.[1]

If you want a responsible partner who can commit to a job, pay his bills, and so on, look for the above qualities.

If a man objects to any talk about whether he's hoping to marry, he's probably not ready for marriage. To test the waters, I suggest that you talk directly to someone you like before allowing yourself to get too emotionally involved with him. There are different ways to approach this sensitive topic. Depending on the vibes at the moment, you might casually say something like, "I'm wondering whether you want a friend or if you're, in general, looking for a marriage partner." Only you know how long you're willing to wait to find out. You might feel okay asking very casually on the second or third date, or possibly a bit later. You want to use your dating time wisely, don't you?

## Signs That He's Not for You

If he says he doesn't want to marry, believe him and move on. But even if he does want to, make sure the answers to questions like these are a clear *no*:

- Does he spend irresponsibly?
- Does he speak negatively about marriage?
- Does he hurt you by being unreliable or abusive—or by lying, cheating, or flirting with other women?

Watch out for the above red flags. If you want a good husband, know that a *yes* to any of these questions is a likely disqualifier, even if he's charming and says he loves you. Remember that you are terrific. You deserve and will find someone who recognizes your worth and has the qualities you need for a fulfilling marriage.

If you lack self-confidence, you may be blind to traits that should be deal breakers. If you find yourself staying in a relationship with someone who devalues you, therapy can help you gain self-awareness, self-respect, and assurance that you deserve a partner with whom you feel good about yourself.

## Testing for Long-Term Compatibility

When your relationship begins to feel serious, talk about what your lives together would look like after marriage. Even many couples who cohabited first say that marriage changes the relationship.

So discuss together how you want your married life to be. Say what matters to each of you. Maybe my husband sensed that I wasn't cut out for a traditional gender-based division of responsibilities. One evening while we sat on my living room couch, well before we got engaged, he said, "I'm not the kind of guy who expects his wife to have dinner on the table at a certain time each evening."

Green light for me. I could be myself with David. Being able to be yourself with a future husband is a crucial thing to test for, along with good chemistry and character traits, similar values, and enough shared interests. If you're also both marriage minded, comfortable being yourselves with each other, and able to accept your differences, you can look forward to a real-life happily ever after.

# THERAPY

Good therapy has helped countless women succeed in marriage. Often we can get in our own way without knowing it. Ambivalence about marrying can cause us to stay involved with someone who won't commit or reject someone who will. For various reasons, a woman may become involved with a man or series of men who lack qualities essential for her happiness. After experiencing such a relationship or unhappy marriage, she may become bitter and cynical about committing.

Lana used to pine after men who weren't interested in marriage and reject those who were. She was conflicted about marrying because she'd never recovered from the shock of her parents' divorce when she was thirteen. Her mother's words echoed through Lana's teen years: "I gave him the best years of my life, and he left me for another woman."

## Reversing a Pattern

Lana eventually recognized her pattern. Still longing for marriage, she was finally ready to get therapy. Had she not made that commitment, Jules, a shy, kind, marriage-minded man, would have been beneath her radar. When she complained to her therapist about Jules's faults, he said, "There you go again." Lana came to realize that her criticisms weren't deal breakers; they were more about her own insecurities. She feared that, like her mother, she too would be tragically disappointed if she married.

Therapy helped Lana transform her fear of failure into confidence that she would succeed. She and Jules have now been happily married for over thirty years. If you genuinely want to marry and something's been holding you back, therapy can help you grow personally and create the kind of relationship and life you truly want.

## How to Choose a Therapist

Do you view therapists as larger-than-life experts who know what's best for you? The good ones help you to discover this for yourself. If you are considering psychotherapy, think about what qualities you value in a therapist. Do you think a man or a woman will be more helpful for you? Someone from a similar cultural, religious, or spiritual background to your own?

In the above example, Lana hoped to marry someone who, like her, was Jewish and wanted children. She collected the names of some recommended professionals. Of the five therapists she'd interviewed by phone, she met with two of them in person.

Lana knew that her parents' divorce and its aftermath were causing her to reject marriage-minded men. She sensed that a Jewish male therapist, who was still married to his original wife and had successfully raised children to adulthood, would be best for her. Lana wanted an excellent therapist who was also a trustworthy husband and father, not someone like her father who'd left a wife and children. One of the therapists matched her criteria. He was kind, insightful, and a good listener. She chose him and continued to see him after marrying and becoming a mother.

## You're Worth It

If you are interested in therapy, make sure that the therapist you're considering is professionally qualified and licensed. Think about what kind of person you believe will be a good fit for you. If possible, don't let money get in your way. Good therapy could well be the best investment you'll ever make in yourself.

# TRAUMA

Trauma happens. It's not something people often talk about. Possibly, someone you've been getting to know and like has experienced a horrific life-changing event. It may have been a sudden death or suicide of a close friend or family member, physical or sexual abuse, bullying, violence (domestic or family, war or political), a life-threatening illness, or something else.

Healing takes both time and a willingness to face the trauma, whether it's old, recent, large, or small. We cannot force readiness to deal with trauma. Each of us has our own timetable, which should be respected.

## The Power of Empathic Listening

The best thing you can do as a relationship partner is listen when the trauma survivor is ready to talk. We can't overestimate the power of simply being there for another person, showing quiet empathy. Encouraging remarks such as "That must have been so hard for you to have gone through" or "I hear you saying this is hard for you right now" show empathy.

He (or she) may fear he has burdened or disturbed you by talking about his experience. He's likely to feel relieved and validated if you thank him for sharing it with you.

However, if you find that hearing graphic details about a trauma victim's experience is too overwhelming, permit yourself to explain this to the person sensitively. Many therapists specialize in helping trauma survivors. You might want to encourage the person to seek professional support to recover from trauma.

## Therapy Can Support Recovery

Various therapy approaches help people recover from trauma. EMDR (Eye Movement Desensitization and Reprocessing) helps many people heal from the emotional distress resulting from disturbing life experiences. People also benefit from telling their story to a skilled therapist who validates them for having survived and for coping with their challenges. They can gain a sense of wellness and the ability to move forward in life.

## How Trauma Affects Close Relationships

If a past traumatic event haunts someone with whom you're involved—or if you are being affected similarly—the strain can cause an avoidance of or decrease in emotional or physical intimacy, isolation, feelings of frustration, anger, confusion, sadness, or anxiety. Partners may feel helpless, argue more frequently, and find it difficult to resolve problems.

## How to Respond Constructively

It's easy to take these behaviors personally. Even if you're feeling frustrated, avoid criticizing or complaining. It's better to view the stressed person's actions as symptoms of a disease from which he hasn't yet adequately healed.

You may want to "cure" him right now, but that's not possible. So accept that you cannot fix him. Also, you might find yourself making assumptions about how the person wants to relate to you. Doing so can put the two of you at odds with each other.

It's much better to ask him how he feels about whatever you think he might want to do. For example, you might ask if he feels like taking a walk with you, sitting quietly with you, or making space for himself by doing something alone.

## Do You Need to Heal?

The need to heal may also apply to you. Hearing about a relationship partner's trauma might bring forth feelings about a trauma you've experienced. But put yourself aside while listening to him so you can be fully present. Your story will be for another conversation.

Ideally, healing should be well on the way before you commit to marriage. You don't want a lifelong relationship with a partner whose symptoms turn your life upside down. But it's never too late to recover from trauma. You'll be much happier with someone who's processed enough of his trauma to be a kind, loving partner. Suppose you are still experiencing the aftermath of a traumatic event in your own life, which may be affecting your ability to create a good relationship. In that case, this could be the time for you to arrange for the healing that's needed.

# TRUST

Good marriages are built on a foundation of trust. How do you know if you can trust someone? Trust takes time. It's based on noticing how a person behaves, especially regarding keeping agreements, doing what he says he'll do. Another form of trust involves believing in yourself, feeling confident that you deserve and can create a good marriage.

## Keeping Agreements Builds Trust

Does he keep agreements? Does he make promises and also fulfill them? Is he often late without letting you know? Does he say he wants a serious relationship with you, yet he's involved with someone else?

Although keeping agreements builds trust, we can sometimes allow for a little wiggle room because no one is perfect. Most of us might consider lateness too minor a matter to stress over. However, virtually everyone views infidelity as a major violation of trust.

Intuition may help, but it's naive to trust someone instinctively. We earn trust by behaving honestly, reliably, and responsibly. In the early stage of dating, most people are on their best behavior. By dating someone for about six months or longer before considering marriage, you're more likely to see how both of you are when you let your guard down.

Some marriages based on love at first sight work out well, but most don't. The initial strong attraction is usually based on fantasy and hormones. Consequently, a big letdown can occur after tying the knot too soon, when the real person emerges. He may turn out not to be trustworthy or have another serious character flaw.

## Angie Lacks Trust in Herself

Angie, an attractive nurse in her mid-thirties, dated Dennis for several months. When it looked like the relationship could become serious, she started criticizing him for being too passive and ended the relationship. When she heard that he'd started dating Linda, Angie had second thoughts. She asked Dennis to meet her for lunch. "No, I don't think so," he said.

Dennis married Linda, who loves and accepts him as he is.

Angie is still single because she doesn't trust that she can succeed in marriage. She never got over the loss of her father, who died in a car accident when she was twelve. As an adult, she said she wanted marriage but rejected suitable men because there was always something "wrong" with them. She's played it safe by staying single, avoiding the risk of abandonment and heartbreak again.

If, like Angie, we've been disappointed in a big way by someone we trusted who was significant in our life, we may unconsciously fear commitment. By recognizing a self-defeating pattern, we can take steps to grow personally and succeed in marriage. (See Therapy, page 167.)

## Lack of Role Models Can Hamper Trust

Some women have difficulty trusting that they can have a good marriage because they witnessed a dysfunctional parental relationship while growing up. It's not unusual for them to repeat the experience by being drawn unconsciously to men with whom they can act out roles they viewed as children. For example, a woman who grew up with an angry, critical father might be attracted to this type of man unthinkingly. What's familiar can be oddly comforting when the man's negativity resembles one's parent's. After being in this sort of toxic situation for some time, she may not trust that she can have a good marriage with anyone.

Therapy helps many people move past trust-eroding experiences and gain confidence in their ability to choose a partner wisely and succeed in marriage.

# U is for

○ **Ultimatum**
○ **Unfinished Business**

## ULTIMATUM

Suppose you believe he's the one. But he hasn't proposed. At some point, you'll need to know if he wants to marry you. The conversation is essential. Your time is too precious to spend in a going-nowhere relationship.

Although the word *ultimatum* might sound rough in the context of a romantic relationship, the discussion should be gentle. Initiate it when you're both feeling relaxed and in a good mood.

### When's the Right Time for an Ultimatum?

There is no hard and fast rule for when to give an ultimatum. It should not happen too early or too late. Too early means you haven't known each other long enough to recognize each other's strengths and imperfections. You'll want to go into marriage with both eyes open, not blinded by a fantasy that either the person is perfect or will change according to your wishes.

Too late, though, means that you've let an uncommitted relationship drag on longer than it should. If someone doesn't want to commit, you'll have wasted time that should have been spent with someone who wants marriage.

Your goal is to find out whether he's ready to get engaged. He might feel put on the spot and need time to process his feelings about making such an important life decision. Or he may have some other reason for not answering right away. That's okay as long as you'll get the clarity you need within a reasonable amount of time.

Below are two stories of women who gave an ultimatum after having gotten to know the man well enough over time to believe that he'd be right for them.

## Ruth's Gentle Ultimatum

After Ruth had been seeing Charlie for about six months, she knew she wanted to marry him. The chemistry felt right. She liked being with him, and he had all the qualities she wanted in a husband.

After lunch at a pizzeria on a Sunday afternoon, she and Charlie lingered at their table. The place was nearly empty; no one would overhear them. Here's their conversation:

**Ruth:** Is it okay if I bring up a sensitive topic?
**Charlie:** (*Looking slightly wary*) Err . . . okay.
**Ruth:** I've been wondering if you've been thinking about where our relationship is going.
**Charlie:** (*Sounding receptive*) I've been thinking about it, but I need more time to know for sure.
**Ruth:** (*Nods and smiles, asks softly*) When do you expect to know?
**Charlie:** In two weeks.
**Ruth:** (*Thinks that's reasonable.*) That's fine.

Both Ruth and Charlie know that an ultimatum has been given. Without spelling it out, Ruth has let him know that she will end the relationship if he doesn't commit.

Ruth can speak this way because she truly believes that she will be married, if not to Charlie, then to someone else. A week later, Charlie proposed.

Ruth felt ready to commit to Charlie in six months. For others, it could be about that amount of time or longer. The main idea is for you to know him well enough to believe that you can create a lasting, fulfilling marriage together.

## Irene's Ultimatum

Irene, thirty-eight, and Craig, forty, were both Jewish. Craig considered Irene's stricter level of religious observance a deal breaker. Yet he felt connected to her and continued to date her on and off. Craig had been divorced twice and had two children from his first marriage. He felt conflicted about committing again. Irene knew she wanted marriage.

Their dating followed a pattern. Craig would invite her to his place and cook dinner for the two of them. He'd end it after a few months, saying they were too different in practicing their religion.

After missing Irene for a while, he'd call her again. Again they'd date for a few months, and then he'd tell her it was over. After a couple of years of this on-again, off-again relationship, Irene felt frustrated enough to give an ultimatum.

The last time Craig asked her to date him again, she said, "This time, it has to be *real*." He understood that Irene meant dating had to be with the intention to marry. She added, "And you have to take me on a real date once a week for dinner at a restaurant. If we break up again," she said, "we will never see each other again."

Craig said okay and kept his word. A few weeks later, over crème brûlée at a French restaurant, he surprised Irene, saying, "Let's pick a date."

# UNFINISHED BUSINESS

Do you have "unfinished business" that could be getting in your way of committing to marry? For example, many adults continue to feel angry or hurt by how they were treated by a parent or someone else when they were young. Others may be holding onto unresolved feelings from a problematic past relationship.

These are examples of unfinished business.

Might you be continuing to experience complicated unprocessed feelings from childhood? It's never too late to do what's needed to gain the kind of closure that allows you to accept whatever painful experience you endured as a way to gain understanding, self-awareness, and personal growth.

If your unfinished business involves a former relationship partner who disappointed you, he may have done so because of his own unprocessed issues. However, your focus should be on yourself, not as a victim but as a learner. What new self-understanding can you gain? How will that knowledge guide you to choose a new relationship partner more wisely or create a better relationship with an existing partner?

Attend to any unfinished business from a past relationship that may affect your ability to succeed in a current or future one.

## How Couples Can Prevent Accumulating Unfinished Business

Because unfinished business can block the flow of loving feelings, it's essential to recognize when this is happening in a marriage. My book *Marriage Meetings for Lasting Love: 30 Minutes a Week to the Relationship You've Always Wanted* tells, step by step, how to communicate in ways that prevent misunderstandings and address differences constructively. Spouses don't build grudges, so romance and intimacy can flourish.

If you find that you are continuing to struggle with unfinished business, therapy can help. (See Therapy, page 167.) A skilled, objective professional can guide you toward gaining closure about what's been holding you back. Through this process, you're likely to grow personally and create more satisfying relationships, and a lasting, fulfilling marriage.

# Marriage

 **is for**

- ○ **Values**
- ○ **Vitality**
- ○ **Voluntary**
- ○ **Vulnerable**

## VALUES

It's easy to take our values for granted. Values are the core beliefs that guide our everyday lives. Couples in successful marriages typically share enough of them for long-term compatibility.

If you value honesty, fidelity, a sense of humor, personal growth, respect, empathy, and patience, can you imagine having a life partner who doesn't? How important is it that he be ambitious, open to having children or accepting yours, or in favor of a lifestyle similar to the one you want?

You don't need to agree on everything; the idea is to decide what's truly necessary for your lasting happiness. Sometimes a difference in a core value can enrich a relationship, as described below.

## Complementary Values Can Enhance a Relationship

Jodi and Kevin came to see me for marriage counseling. "I wonder whether Kevin and I are mismatched," Jodi said. She describes herself as ambitious and driven.

Kevin has a low-pressure job and likes it that way. Sometimes he surfs on weekdays. As he puts it, "I care more about quality of life than getting ahead. I earn enough to live in a good area and pay my share of the bills."

This sort of difference can be complimentary. If one partner is tense from the pressure at work, it can be comforting to come home to a calm, supportive partner who helps the other unwind.

Jodi values hard work and perseverance, and Kevin prizes a laid-back quality of life. Their fundamental values are unlikely to change. Jodi has been learning to view this difference as a good thing. She appreciates Kevin's calming influence. She realizes that this was one of his qualities that appealed to her when they first met.

But if Jodi's core belief were that her husband *must* be ambitious, she would have resented him for not carrying his weight. Instead, she appreciates how Kevin's easygoing nature complements her driven one in ways that cannot be measured in dollars and cents.

## Identifying Your Core Values

What values do you hold dear? Are you noticing which core beliefs you and an actual or potential relationship partner have in common? Whether your concern is about money, childcare, housework, or something else, only you will know if a specific difference is acceptable or not.

If it's one you can live with, you're likely to be happier if you focus on what's best for the relationship instead of trying to change him or get your way. Don't expect to agree on every single thing. The best you can do when a tolerable yet uncomfortable difference in values shows up is to communicate in ways that respect both of you.

## Exercise

To identify your core values, think about how you'd like to be remembered. When you're feeling calm and relaxed, you might want to try writing your obituary. If this feels uncomfortable, that's not surprising. If you're willing to give it a try, notice what comes up for you. You will have expressed your true guiding principles. This knowledge should help you ask the right questions to learn whether you and a potential marriage partner are likely to be compatible over time.

# VITALITY

Good marriage partners continue to invest energy into their relationship. So make sure to maintain your vitality by doing activities that foster your sense of aliveness.

Endorphins are hormones that make us feel joyful or at ease with the world. Some ways to boost endorphins are exercising alone or in a group (though research shows that exercising in a group is more effective than doing it alone), getting a massage, talking with a friend, playing music, laughing, and even eating chocolate.

The idea is to do things that give you pleasure.

## Exercise

List at least five things you do that increase your feelings of joy, aliveness, and tranquility.

_____

_____

_____

_____

_____

_____

_____

_____

_____

_____

# VOLUNTARY

You cannot love someone and try to control him. Among other things, love means respecting the other's autonomy, his right to rule himself. Your behaviors and those of your partner should be voluntary.

As you talk about the kind of life you want, focus on what fits for both of you. Ideally, before marriage, you'll talk about money, chores and responsibilities, parenting or step-parenting concerns, where you want to live, and so on.

## Do Not Agree to an Unreasonable Demand

Some people agree to a demand, request, or assumption that is not right for them.

What if a man says he'll marry you, but only if you agree to move to his city, allow a relative of his to live with you, or have the kind of wedding he wants but you don't? If you're tempted to give in because you want to marry him, ask yourself, "Am I really okay with this? If not, but I give in to him now, will I hold a grudge against him for a long time?"

Similarly, if you notice yourself trying to force a partner to do something he doesn't want to do, back off. No good will come from his caving in to your demand. He's likely to feel bitter toward you for coercing him.

Collaboration is best, with each of you choosing freely to do what you agree to and respecting each other's choices.

If one of you is consistently giving, or giving in, more than the other, your relationship will probably suffer from the imbalance. When one person gives a bit more in a good friendship, the other will also want to give more. But if one routinely gives less, the other's desire to be generous is likely to decrease. Consequently, the relationship will probably spiral downward and take on a romance-depleting, weighing and measuring, nitpicking character.

You're likely to notice whether the two of you are in harmony about giving. If you feel you're not receiving enough, remember that you have the right to ask for what you want.

### Encouraging Volunteering

But no demands, please. Don't tell your partner what he *must* do. Instead, ask gently for what you'd like to happen. In a good relationship, both of you enjoy giving in a way that respects each other's preferences. If one wants something that the other is not prepared to offer, and the thing isn't a deal breaker, this is okay. Both of you are entitled to have boundaries. (See Boundaries, page 15.)

There may be times when you experience yourself as a victim. When this happens, view it as a wake-up call. It's time for you to take charge. A victim stays stuck, involuntarily, in an unhealthy situation.

You can move forward.

As a volunteer, you can choose your partner wisely. All intimate relationships have ups and downs. Yet you can communicate in ways that foster more romance, intimacy, and teamwork. You can resolve issues respectfully and often smoothly.

# VULNERABLE

In a good marriage, you can be yourself with your partner more than with anyone else in the world. You can have imperfections and still be loved. Being vulnerable means sharing your true self with your partner instead of saying what you think he wants to hear.

According to meditation teacher and author Sharon Salzburg, "Embracing our inherent vulnerability is one of the best ways to break the cycle of fear and self-preoccupation. This can be as simple as accepting help from others when we need it. . . . We think we should be in charge all the time, that we should always be in control . . . it's just not true."

Many men find it especially difficult to reveal their vulnerability. Someone may get fired from his job and delay telling his wife for several days or longer. This is the John Wayne image of an invincible "man's man," who always comes out on top and doesn't express tender feelings, and it persists like the male ego.

A man might fear that if he says what he really feels or thinks or if he acknowledges a shortcoming, you'll think less of him. So when he does open up, be attentive and empathic. For example, if he sounds angry, even if at you, you might say mildly, "I hear you're feeling angry (or upset or hurt)."

## Being Vulnerable Can Feel Risky

When we say what we want and how we feel, we're opening our insides. Some people might empathize and recognize our shared humanity. But others might judge us negatively or tell us that our thoughts or feelings are wrong.

People who have difficulty accepting another person's expression of vulnerability probably find it difficult to air their own thoughts and feelings that they judge unacceptable.

Harold appears earlier in this book, in the Grace entry. After Jenny told him sadly that she was unemployed, he responded by putting her down: "It's too bad that you don't have any skills." If someone shows such an extreme lack of empathy, as Harold does, he is a poor candidate for a good marriage. A supportive person will listen and respond respectfully when you reveal your true self or situation. He'll be kind and accepting, not belittle you.

If you find that someone you're getting to know responds negatively when you reveal vulnerability, you've learned something important: he may not be for you. You want someone who accepts the real you.

## Difficulty Revealing Vulnerability Often Starts in Childhood

Many of my psychotherapy clients have relationship difficulties because they don't communicate authentically. As children, they learned that it could be dangerous to reveal their real thoughts, feelings, or desires.

An angry little girl or boy might tell a parent, "I hate you," and the parent might punish them or say they have a mean streak. The child learns that it's not okay to express anger. A child might say what she wants to do for a vacation and be told by a parent, "You're selfish," so she learns it's not safe to ask for what you want. She learns to hold back on self-expression and carries the pattern into adulthood. She (or he) becomes a people pleaser who is afraid to expose her true self. Instead, she shares only feelings, thoughts, and desires that she thinks are acceptable.

## Revealing Vulnerability Brings Relationship Rewards

By relating vulnerably, you and your relationship partner get to know and understand each other more deeply. Allowing others to see our vulnerability also permits the other person to empathize with us and sometimes help us out, which is how a good spouse responds to a partner's openness.

If you and a potential marriage partner find it difficult to be vulnerable, consider seeking counseling to improve your ability to connect more meaningfully.

# W is for

o  **Wedding**

## WEDDING

Mia found wedding planning stressful. Her mother was obsessing over the invitations, flowers, color scheme, favors, hors d'oeuvres, guest list, and other details—so much that it seemed like *she* was the one getting married.

Exasperated as her mother droned on about ice sculptures and chocolate fountains, Mia began to wish she were eloping. She finally blurted out: "It's not the wedding, Mom. It's the *marriage!*"

Many couples mix up their priorities. They stage elaborate, over-the-top weddings, thinking they're fostering a wonderful marriage. Yet research reveals that the most expensive weddings typically result in the shortest marriages.

David and I had two weddings. Along the way, we learned a couple of things about creating a good marriage.

First, we set a wedding date and venue at the Reform synagogue I'd belonged to. We're both Jewish, but our observance was mostly cultural at the time—bagels and lox, that sort of thing. But after a couple of required premarriage counseling sessions with the synagogue's rabbi, I realized I wanted a different kind of wedding.

A couple of months earlier, I attended a private home wedding officiated by a Chabad (Orthodox) rabbi. I'd never seen anything like it. It felt so holy and spiritual. I realized that I wanted this kind of wedding.

How could we suddenly change everything? David asked. We'd already arranged for catering. The invitations were printed and ready to send. But his main objection was that our families and friends would feel uncomfortable at a Chabad-style wedding. Chabad rabbis typically have long beards. They wear black fedoras and black frock coats at synagogues and formal events like weddings. They practice Judaism without compromise, observing both the spirit and letter of its laws. David didn't want to subject our friends and family to something so unfamiliar and extreme.

I didn't know what to do.

Then I thought of Rabbi Rabinowitz, the Skolye Rebbe from Brooklyn. When I first met David, Rabbi Rabinowitz was in California. I consulted with him privately regarding my insecurities about marrying. He'd said, "Marriage will be the best thing for you." When I looked surprised, he added, "Your marriage will be 97 percent successful." I felt disappointed, and wished he'd said 100 percent.

Rabbi Rabinowitz said I could phone him anytime and that he remembers everything. So I phoned him to ask what to do about the conflict David and I were having. He said, "One likes chocolate; the other likes vanilla. Have both."

So we had both. First, we had a small Chabad wedding, self-catered with a kosher deli lunch in a private home. Over a hundred relatives and friends joined us for the ceremony and celebration at the Reform synagogue seven weeks later.

"It's not the wedding; it's the marriage." To keep the relationship on track, partners need to stay resourceful to create win-win solutions that satisfy both people. That's the key to creating a 97 percent successful marriage—not a fairy-tale-based 100 percent blissful one, but a real-life marriage, with ups and downs that's still pretty great.

#  X is for

- ○ E**X**asperating
- ○ E**X**citing
- ○ E**X**es
- ○ E**X**pectations (for Marriage)

## E**X**ASPERATING

Rabbi Rabinowitz had predicted that my marriage would be 97 percent successful. (See Wedding, page 186.) I think he understood that I held a fairytale–based, all-or-nothing expectation about marriage. I thought if it wasn't perfect, then it was a failure.

I think he wanted me to feel assured my marriage would be fine but not blissful all the time. He understood that if we expect our marriage to be a nonstop happily-ever-after experience, we'll be in for a huge letdown.

Even in the best marriages, sometimes spouses get frustrated with each other. In fulfilling unions, they learn to appreciate each other's virtues and accept and adjust to their imperfections. Yet often, this acceptance follows some wondering how they could have wed such an incompetent, arrogant, passive, lazy, careless, sloppy, inconsiderate, or _____ (you can fill in the blank for your pet peeve) person.

When I was single and naive enough to think marriage success meant being nonstop crazy-in-love with your spouse, I shared a table at a crowded café with a widower in his eighties. He'd had a long, happy marriage. His expression was radiant as he described his feelings about his wife. "When her lateness drove me crazy, I wondered why I married someone so difficult," he said. "Other times, I thought she was absolutely wonderful. I felt so fortunate that she married me."

Exasperation can surface at times in any marriage. When I told a couple in therapy with me that all marriages have ups and downs, the wife let out a huge sigh of relief and said, "Thank you!"

Once you accept that irritations happen in marriage, you can relax and usually enjoy the ride. So take a couple of deep breaths when you're feeling annoyed about something that's not important for your long-term happiness. The feeling is temporary. It will pass.

It often helps to remember what attracted you to him in the first place and still does. Look at the big picture. If you're basically well matched and usually happy together, the frustrations that show up now and then may be upsetting, but they're probably in the range of normal and easier to accept than the sense of incompleteness and loneliness felt by singles who long for a life partner.

# EXCITING

When single, we may yearn for the security of marriage. After it happens, sooner or later, a common complaint is "What happened to romance?"

After marrying, many people lapse into boredom with their partner and their life.

The "he loves me, he loves me not" kind of unpredictability of dating gets replaced in a healthy marriage with a calmer emotional state that comes with a stable, enduring, monogamous relationship.

## Keeping Romance Alive

To help keep the romance flowing, schedule a weekly date with your spouse. You can create excitement with novelty: a new place, an exhilarating sport to engage in or watch, or any out-of-the-ordinary experience.

Your date is a time to daydream out loud or silently. You get away from home and don't talk about chores or issues because the idea is to enjoy being out together, like when you were first getting to know each other.

If you have young children or possibly an elderly relative living with you, you may think you need to stay home. Arranging for a babysitter or short-term care provider can be challenging, but it's worth doing. Persist and be resourceful. Remember that the best gift you can give to your child is a good marriage.

## Personal Growth Is an Adventure

Marriage offers endless possibilities for growth. We discover interesting, sometimes fascinating aspects of ourselves and our spouse. A woman from India, whose happy marriage was an arranged one, described how she and her husband perceive themselves.[1] She said that they don't think of themselves as human beings but as "human becomings."

A good marriage helps us transcend our selfish concerns. Partners become more flexible, tolerant, and generous. We do not lose our identity as individuals. Instead, we tune into our needs and learn to express them positively and respectfully, which can feel like an adventure in itself.

I'm privileged to see this process happen in couples in my psychotherapy practice. They usually start out blaming each other for whatever is amiss in their relationship. Sooner or later, each spouse recognizes their contribution to the situation and takes responsibility for relating more positively. They gain acceptance of their own and their partner's imperfections. Intimacy grows.

This kind of progress is more likely to happen in marriage than in other relationships. If you take your marriage vows seriously, you are likely to cope better during the rough times, find solutions, and grow good character traits. Like the Indian couple, you may come to view yourselves as human becomings.

## Add Unpredictability to Shared Experiences

What might the two of you do to add more uncertainty, unpredictability, and fun? Be open to doing something different even if you feel resistant initially, which is natural when veering off a long-established way of vacationing, for example.

If you need ideas for what to do on a date, think back to activities you enjoyed when you were children, young adults, and first getting to know each other. You can also gain ideas by searching online for "lists of pleasurable activities."

## Make Sure to Go *Out*

Watching a movie at home isn't a date. Too many reminders of pending chores are present. The idea is to go out where you forget about all that. Your date can be a walk or hike in the woods, a beach outing, or a concert in a park. It could mean going out for a casual meal or to an elegant restaurant. Dressing up for special occasions enhances your attractiveness to each other.

Add the element of unpredictability on dates and vacations with whatever floats your boat literally on local waters or on a cruise ship—or by skiing, flying kites, camping, skating, or anything else that takes you away from your everyday lives. And do keep learning. How about attending a lecture or taking a class together?

## Keep Having Sex

Satisfying sex is exciting. Yet life's busyness can leave us too tired or preoccupied to be in the mood. Many couples schedule a weekly time for sex when they're likely to be available and in the mood. Spontaneous sex is lovely. Setting a time for sex doesn't rule out other times; it's a way to keep sex from getting lost in the shuffle of your busy lives.

Sex doesn't need to happen at the arranged time. But if you're getting along well, you'll look forward to the rendezvous. The main thing is to keep good sex happening. It's like a glue that keeps you connected romantically, emotionally, and spiritually.

If you're going through a time when you're not getting along well, you may feel too distant emotionally to want to have sex. This is why it's essential to clear up any misunderstandings or tell your partner what's getting in the way for you. If necessary, consider seeing a professional who can help the two of you reconnect and get back on track.

# EXES

Some exes want to end all contact; others don't. If either of you has a former marriage or romantic partner, it's important to clarify that relationship's status.

If children are in the picture, you can learn more about approaching parenting and step-parenting concerns sensitively by reading about the topic and talking to others who've successfully navigated similar relationships.

Some ex-partners want to see each other as friends. They may like to get together in person or send texts or email messages. Their continuing contact can feel threatening to a new spouse. It's important to clarify what will work for you and your current partner and set boundaries with which you both can live.

A couple might agree that neither of them will get together with an ex-partner privately or at all. Or they might decide to include the new partner in their interactions.

## Jennifer Sets a Boundary

Jennifer became aware that her husband, Jordan, was exchanging emails with Sherri, a married woman he'd known when both were single. He wasn't secretive; he'd forwarded to Jennifer an email from Sherri that hinted she was having marital issues.

Jennifer felt uncomfortable about these emails and told her husband, "I don't think it's good for our relationship if one of us has a private relationship with someone of the opposite sex. It makes me uncomfortable. If you want to stay in touch with her, how about including me in all conversations?" The emails stopped.

Jennifer was asking for transparency. Doing so can be a solution, or something different might work for you. Every spouse wants to feel like they are number one. Take good care of your current relationship. Don't do anything on the sly. If both of you do what's best for your relationship, your connection will thrive.

# EXPECTATIONS (FOR MARRIAGE)

Many people marry and soon find that their spouse is annoying, not always but more than expected. Fairy tales and romantic novels suggest that a good marriage is an effortless, happily-ever-after experience.

A good marriage provides companionship, comfort, security, emotional intimacy, sex, and a sense of completion. We feel whole and more at home with our spouse.

But don't let fairy tales and romantic movies and novels confuse you. Naive expectations cause us to feel shortchanged. By keeping your beliefs realistic, you're much more likely to appreciate your partner's good qualities and your marriage.

The chart on the next page shows how to change some common unrealistic expectations for marriage into relationship-enhancing ones.

# WHAT DO YOU EXPECT FROM MARRIAGE?

| *Unrealistic Expectations* | *Realistic Expectations* |
| --- | --- |
| It will be easy to transition from single to married. | Getting married is a significant change. It takes time to adjust to your new roles and each other. |
| I'll never be lonely again. | One person cannot satisfy all your needs for companionship. Maintain friendships with others. |
| I won't be bored anymore. | You are responsible for keeping yourself entertained and interesting. It's not your spouse's job. |
| We'll never argue. | Conflicts occur in close relationships. You can learn to manage them well. |
| He'll change after we're married in the ways I want him to. | "What you see is what you get." Don't expect your partner to change established character traits or habits. |
| He'll know how I feel and what I want; I shouldn't need to tell him. | He can't read your mind. If you want him to know something, tell him. |
| Marriage is a 50-50 proposition. | It's better to give and receive graciously than to get all even-steven about what's "fair." |
| He'll do chores the way I want them done. | His standards and ways are likely to be different from yours. It's best to accept this. |
| Sex will always be great. | Sex should often be great, but it won't be every single time. Good communication helps here too. |

If you hold some of the expectations on the left side of the chart, join the crowd. Such beliefs are widespread. In my therapy practice, I see the damage they create in marriages. I also see the transformation that occurs when spouses lower their expectations and become more accepting of themselves and each other.

The mind-reading expectation is an example of a particularly harmful one because it often results in misunderstandings and hurt feelings. A spouse thinks, *Why doesn't he do what I want (or know how I feel)? I shouldn't have to tell him.*

It's not realistic and can be harmful to expect your spouse to read your mind. A wife who's disappointed with her husband for not sensing her needs is likely to become resentful and act out her feelings. She might give him the silent treatment or withhold sex. A husband who's angry at his wife for not knowing what he wants might withdraw and sulk. Grudges build, and the relationship becomes compromised over time.

What if the wife in this example realizes that it's unreasonable to expect her husband to read her mind? She now tells herself, *If I want him to know what I feel, think, or need, I have to* tell *him.* And then she does express herself clearly and compassionately.

By stating our feelings, wants, and needs directly and respectfully to our partner, we increase understanding and strengthen our connection. By changing unrealistic expectations about marriage into more sensible ones, we become more accepting of our mate and foster a happier, more fulfilling marriage.

#  is for

○ **You**

## YOU

*The longest relationship we have with anyone is with ourselves, and yet that relationship is often the first one we let slide. Maintaining it brings such comfort, though: liking your company means that you always have at your beck and call a person who gets you.*

—ROBIN ROMM

When you marry, you bring your unique self into the relationship. Your spouse married you because he cherishes you being *you*.

Many women, and some men, get married and forget who they are. They may believe the "togetherness" myth suggests that two become one in a way that causes them to lose their separate identity.

In general, women are naturally more empathic than men. Consequently, they're more likely to intuit their partner's wants and needs and try to meet them, sometimes ignoring the cost to themselves.

A woman may dislike football, crowds, and noise, yet she'll endure many Sundays at stadiums *together* because she thinks a good marriage requires this. She might visit his parents much more frequently than she sees her parents because that's what her husband wants. She might teeter in painful spiky high heels because he likes how sexy she looks in them.

## Marital Relationship as a Braid

Earlier, I mentioned that Amy described her marriage as a three-stranded braid. One strand is herself, another is Michael, and the third is their relationship. Amy and Michael understand that being in a relationship means connecting, not clinging. She loves to travel. He'd rather stay home and practice karate. So Amy travels with a woman friend, and he's okay with that.

Michael and Amy are sensitive to and considerate of each other. They enjoy their time together. By pursuing their separate interests, they stay vibrant and attractive. Self-care is not selfish.

## Losing and Finding Balance

If you try to stand on one foot for as long as you can, at some point you will lose your balance. You'll need to put down the other foot to regain it. We feel similarly off-kilter when we forget to nurture our separate identity, which we need to maintain to feel fully supported.

A spouse who gets into a pattern of placating her partner may feel okay at first. But eventually, she'll feel resentful about being a doormat. If this sounds like you, stop denying your needs. To get back to the calm, relaxed center that exists deep within all of us, ask yourself, "What has to happen for me to feel better?" Then do your best to make that occur.

It's easy to lose track of ourselves. Self-nurturing activities help us reconnect with our inner selves. Taking a bath, walking alone or maybe with a friend, making a painting, and writing in a journal are just a few ways people take time for themselves. By engaging in them, your mind can daydream or wander freely, and you're likely to feel revived and optimistic.

Using positive communication techniques also helps us restore balance. Be willing to stand up for and to speak up about what's important to you. (See Negotiate, page 111.)

## Marriage Meetings Restore Balance

A marriage meeting is a short, gentle, loosely structured conversation that keeps your relationship on track while honoring each of your unique selves. *Marriage Meetings for Lasting Love: 30 Minutes a Week to the Relationship You've Always Wanted* tells, step by step, how to hold a marriage meeting, using a simple, easy-to-follow format and positive communication skills. (See Marriage Meetings, page 88.)

Effective marriage meetings foster romance, intimacy, teamwork, and smoother resolutions of issues. My husband and I have been holding them for over thirty years. I give them major credit for our lasting happiness.

# Z is for

- ○ Zest
- ○ Zzz (Sleep)

## ZEST

Have you heard that marriages can become boring? The relationship can start to feel ho-hum when things have gotten too predictable, but you can do something about it.

Routines are needed, but this doesn't mean that the thrills have to end. By trying out some different activities from your usual ones, you'll enjoy the comfort of the familiar and also add excitement.

### Zest Is Contagious

By engaging in activities that bring a sense of joie de vivre, you sparkle. Your aliveness is contagious. It will spice things up for both of you. So take a break from a routine and do something else, even if it doesn't feel comfortable at first.

When my husband and I vacationed in Hawaii a long time ago, we went to most places with our toddler son. We also each went on an outing individually while the other stayed with him.

Although David occasionally plays golf near home, playing on a sunny course in Maui, dotted with palm trees and overlooking the ocean, was something else!

The next day was my turn. I took a snorkeling cruise, entering the water near a coral reef where one school of fish after another, striped, speckled, and iridescent, glided near me. I felt immersed in a mystical experience.

## Helicopter over Maui

The next day, my husband said he wanted to do something exciting as a family, create a memory. He suggested splurging on a helicopter tour of the island. Up we went with our small son between us, with mufflers on our ears to mute the engine's noise. We viewed the massive Haleakalā volcano from above. At one point, the pilot headed toward a cliff, bluffing us into thinking we were about to crash. As we held our breaths, he maneuvered the plane to clear it. He knew what he was doing; his job is to thrill tourists. He gave us an unforgettable if hair-raising experience.

Our son, now an adult, was too young back then to remember that Hawaiian vacation, but my husband and I still have vivid memories of doing what thrilled each of us there, together and on our own.

## You Can Gain Zest Near Home

You don't need to go far from home to gain zest. You can learn a new sport, get a pet, act in a play, fly a kite, or explore any one of countless possibilities. Here are a few more ideas:

- a romantic dinner at home
- a walk in the woods or elsewhere
- a picnic
- a movie, play, or concert
- a horseback ride

The opportunities to give your relationship a lift are out there. We owe it to ourselves to keep the zest alive.

# ZZZ (SLEEP)

Marriage is not a sprint—a quick trip to the altar or chuppah[1] and then you're done. Marriage is a marathon, a lifelong adventure. It requires an ongoing balancing act to respect your own and your spouse's needs, preferences, and quirks. To succeed, do your best to stay in top shape emotionally and physically.

Do you notice how much more relaxed and all-around better you feel after getting a good night's sleep—like you can take on the world? With too little sleep, we're likely to become dull, tense, or impatient. We may become overly sensitive to a perceived slight when none is intended. Getting enough rest is a big plus. Nap, if necessary, to stay fresh and vibrant as a partner.

You may want to consult your physician if getting enough sleep is a concern. You can gain ideas for better sleep on the internet, in books, and elsewhere.

Ideally, you'll bring your best functioning, thoughtful, constructive self to your relationship with your partner and others every day, regardless of life's ups and downs. So do make sure to get enough sleep.

# Conclusion

*Your task is not to seek for love, but merely to seek and find all the barriers within yourself that you have built against it.*

—RUMI

In a successful relationship today, spouses respect each other and also transcend their separate selves. The result is a beautiful whole that is greater than the sum of its parts and nourishes both partners.

Yes, it can feel challenging to create such a union. While real life is different from what fairy tales say, creating a fulfilling marriage is easier than you may think.

The first thing to do is to let go of the popular notion that to find your life partner, all you need to do is follow your heart.

Don't get me wrong. Your feelings count and can help guide you along your journey toward a lasting, fulfilling marriage. Of course, a mutual attraction should be there, and you should feel good about yourself and accepted and treasured by the one who's for you. You'll be happiest with someone with whom you can relax and be yourself.

So do listen to your heart. But keep your brain in charge of your decisions because feelings can be short-lived when there is no basis for getting along well over time. Look for enough compatibility in values, intelligence, interests, and lifestyle preferences.

Couples who are well-matched do not need to keep "working" on their marriage to keep it sound. In a good marriage, spouses invest energy into their relationship. They learn how to keep it thriving and put what they've learned into practice. That doesn't feel like work; it's how treasured friends relate.

So, where does the idea come from that couples need to "work" on their relationship? Perhaps it comes from the "follow your heart" folks who marry someone they find attractive initially but with whom they lack essential commonalities. In such a union, one frustrated spouse continually labors in a losing battle, trying to change the other because they cannot accept some fundamental differences.

However, couples who are compatible may also feel like they are working on their relationship because they haven't learned to use tools and techniques to keep it thriving almost effortlessly, at least most of the time.

The knowledge is out there and accessible via reading, classes, workshops, and mentors. In *Marriage Meetings for Lasting Love: 30 Minutes a Week to the Relationship You've Always Wanted*, I encourage a proactive approach for long-term happiness. Effective marriage meetings increase intimacy, romance, and teamwork, and they help resolve issues more smoothly.

*Marriage Minded* begins with dating and continues beyond the wedding because it's not the wedding that should be center stage; it's the marriage. Enjoy your journey toward success, and welcome the challenges and joys you'll find along the way.

# Appendix

## Class Handout for
## *Marry With Confidence Workshop*

## Part 1: Overcoming Obstacles

**Guidelines, Introductions, Expectations**

<u>Exercise #1:</u> Group identifies external and internal obstacles to marrying.

<u>Exercise #2:</u> Attitude identification.
What do you tell yourself about marriage, whether regarding your worthiness of a good husband, what may go wrong in your marriage, or something else?
    A. Write your marriage goal.
    B. What is your current attitude around achieving this goal?
    C. What is your desired attitude?

**Exercise #3: Know what you're looking for.**

List ten qualities you desire in a husband. Then share (optional) your list with another class participant. Evaluate your list by separating needs (deal breakers when absent) from wants.

1. _____

_____

2. _____

_____

3. _____

_____

4. _____

_____

5. _____

_____

6. _____

_____

7. _____

_____

8. _____

_____

9. _____

_____

10. _____

**Exercise #4: Know you have lots to offer.**

List ten strengths (good traits you possess) you expect to contribute to your marriage, which your husband-to-be will likely appreciate.

1. _____

_____

2. _____

_____

3. _____

_____

4. _____

5. _____

6. _____

7. _____

8. _____

9. _____

10. _____

## Exercise #5: Who's perfect?

List up to five qualities in yourself that could use some improvement—from a potential husband's viewpoint.

1. _____

2. _____

3. _____

4. _____

5. _____

## Exercise # 6: Identify your goals.

Thinking about your life, *aside from marrying*, what do you want to accomplish in the next year? If you'd like to try the same exercise for five years or longer, use a time framework or combination that fits for you.

1. _____

2. _____

3. _____

# Part 2: How to Date[1]

### Pre-Dating Requirements, Questions to Ask Yourself

- Do I have any physiological or other issues that would hinder me from developing a trusting, intimate relationship?
- Can I do something about it currently?
- Why do I want to get married?
- What advantages to being single am I aware of?
- Do I have a list of benefits of exchanging singlehood for attachment?
- Do I have a portrait of self-identity? Do I have strong points (positive qualities) of which I'm aware? Are these the same points I want others to notice immediately?

*Remember:* The purpose of dating is to ascertain whether the person is a suitable marriage partner. Therefore, every date that leads you closer to that information is a successful date.

### Dating Tips

1. **On the first two or three dates, keep the conversation light and maintain enough physical and emotional distance to assess the following:**
- Am I comfortable with his physical presence?
- Am I comfortable being myself with him?

2. **Love at first sight is usually infatuation, which fades. "Like" at first sight is a better predictor for a future.** The

best predictor is whether you still like each other after about three months of seeing each other regularly.

3. **Some preliminary information, to explore as soon as is practical before or on early dates, includes his**
   - approximate age;
   - profession;
   - interests and hobbies ("What do you do for fun?" is an excellent first date question.);
   - level of religious commitment and affiliation;
   - affiliations with organizations;
   - family status (parents, siblings, previous marital and family history);
   - personal preferences;
   - friends and acquaintances; and
   - readiness to commit to marriage (in general, not specifically to you)—discuss in a light, casual, conversational way.

4. **Further dates**: Am I developing an attraction toward this man? Would I consider this a developing friendship? Would I want to get to know this person in an intimate way? Consider keeping a journal to record your feelings and impressions.

5. **Regarding his readiness for marriage, pay attention to his signals**. Is he making you a priority in his life? Introducing you to friends and family? Investing in the relationship in other ways or willing to treat you on dates (if financially feasible)? Letting you know he is attracted to you without trying to pressure you?

6. **Communicating your interest**
   Men marry women who let them know they like and respect them. Women like men around whom they feel good about themselves. So reinforce a man's self-esteem with compliments

such as about what you appreciate and admire about him.
Examples:

*Affirming a lifestyle*
I am impressed with your dedication as a teacher.
I respect you for your decision to _____.

*Affirming the person*
I like the way you express yourself.
I admire your commitment to _____.
I am very impressed with the way you handled that situation.
I appreciate your kindness.

*Expressing the personal impact on yourself*
I feel secure with you.
Your optimism brings out my best qualities.
I am inspired by your _____.

7. **Assessing your feelings**
   *After the first date:*
   - How did he respond to the affirmations?
   - How did I feel about his responses?
   - Is he someone who can accept compliments and return them?
   - How comfortable did I feel with him?
   - Is there anything that prevents me from wanting to date him again?

   *After other dates:*
   - Did he express openness?
   - Was I interested in what he had to say?
   - Did I learn something unexpected?
   - Do I feel I know him better?
   - Am I ready to reveal more about myself?

8. **Expressing your human vulnerability, for example, by saying things like the following:**
   - I realized last night that I owe you an apology. I interrupted you . . .
   - I am sorry I kept you waiting for my call today.
   - Though you haven't mentioned it, I am aware that I have a nervous tic.
   - I have a weight issue.

9. **Appropriate conversational topics**

   Have you ever ended a date wondering, *Did I say too much?* Or, *Why did I tell him that?* While dating, choose topics that will create an accurate impression of yourself and vice versa for your date. Do not reveal everything you ever did in your life that you regret, all the negative attributes you believe about yourself, or the detailed accounts of your past failed dating experiences. The information you choose to reveal should be relevant to the dating stage you are at. Some information is appropriate on a first date; other information is not suitable until much further along in the process.

10. **Examples of topics that are almost always inappropriate on a first date—and typically not appropriate until you and he are serious marriage candidates:**
    - Past failed dating experiences.
    - Your divorce, if applicable. Don't dwell on it. Instead, say, "Yes, I was married for a while, but we divorced two years ago. I learned from that experience and have moved forward." If your date wants more details, say very nicely that, while you have nothing to hide, you don't feel comfortable sharing such personal information at this point.
    - Your embarrassing mistakes and incidents when you are just getting to know him.
    - Your negative character traits.

- The bad day you had today—you got to work late, had a disagreement with your sister, and lost your wallet. Blow off steam with a good friend or family member. Don't put yourself in a situation where you feel compelled to vent during your date.
- Details of your family dynamics. Such information will be important to discuss with any serious marriage candidate. But on a first date, you risk giving or hearing information out of context.

You may want to think about what you will talk about with your date before the date. Consider: Is this topic appropriate for the dating stage we are at, and will it create an accurate impression of who I am? A good question to ask on a first date is, "What do you do for fun?"

11. **Questions you should be asking yourself and warning signs to be aware of while dating:**
    A. Am I sufficiently lonely to drastically change my life for someone else?
    B. Can I acknowledge the faults, including habits and lifestyles I see in my potential mate as they exist now, and still feel comfortable enough to marry him?
    C. Do I feel compromised or threatened now in this relationship?
    D. Am I in love with him, or am I in love with his love for me? *Hint:* As Rabbi Manis Friedman says, don't marry a man because he thinks you're wonderful; marry a man who thinks marriage is wonderful. Why? Because if you marry the first kind, when you stop being wonderful, poof!
    E. Can we respectfully disagree? Am I frightened to disagree with him?
    F. Has he shown support for me?
    G. Do I respect and admire his dreams and aspirations?

H. Am I treated with respect? Does he treat me as an equal? Does he accept my boundaries once I communicate them respectfully?

I. Do I see myself changing, or do I envision the same me?

J. Are my friends and family supportive of this man to whom I want to commit?

K. Does he show signs of being ready and able to commit?

Say no to a relationship that does not feel like a good fit. Do not continue to date such a man; make room for someone who feels right.

## Part 3: Tips to Attract a Good Man

1. **Recognize that you are a good woman!** Own your strengths and vulnerabilities. Accept every part of yourself with love, compassion, and humility.

2. **Keep growing! Set personal and professional goals—aside from marriage.** People who are growing are like lanterns illuminating their surroundings. Good men will be attracted to your light (aliveness).

3. **Know that men marry women in whose presence they feel good about themselves.** Men are incredibly vulnerable. They need to feel accepted, approved of, and loved by a woman. They are dependent on women for their self-esteem, motivation, and drive to achieve.

   So let him know what you like, admire, and find attractive about him while being your sincere self. Be kind and courteous. (It sounds obvious, but when you are worried about how he perceives you or about whether or not he likes you, you may forget.)

4. **Be generally cheerful, and be yourself when with him.** Understand that he wants you to be happy and that he feels good about himself when he's pleasing you. Find out what makes him happy, and let him know when he does something you enjoy. Yet be authentic. Most likely, you won't always feel upbeat. It's okay to share an occasional sad feeling too. Mainly, be your natural, resilient, girl-next-door self. Accept and appreciate him as he is. Be a friend.

5. **Remember to**
   - nurture yourself by pursuing activities and interests you enjoy;
   - make kindness a habit—help and support others;
   - smile often;
   - keep your sense of humor; and
   - live a well-balanced life, as shown in the chart on the next page.

   *The goal:* Get all areas in balance. Look for quantity and balance. Score yourself for each dimension, allowing for a maximum of twenty-five points for each box. Add scores to get your total score. Then draw four labeled circles (as per grid labels), and stack them like a snowman (or snowwoman). Size each circle according to your score for its corresponding box. Decide in which area you need to invest more energy to get yourself more in balance.

# Live the life you love; love the life you live!

## *Self-Care Grid*[2]

### Biological/Physical
- Exercise
- Diet
- Rest
- Toxic substances
- Good medical care
- Financial wellness

### Psychological
- Stress
- A full range of emotions
- A sense of purpose
- Positive thinking
  (Core issues: self-defeating patterns of behavior that continue to sabotage your life. It's essential to have someone to give you feedback, to call you on your "stuff.")

### Social
- Friends—people who lift you or hold you back
- Reciprocal love—needing someone to hold you and say you're okay
- Intimacy
- Support
- Commitment
- Fun
- Solitude—Are you okay with being alone with yourself?

### Spiritual
- Religious honesty
- Spiritual practice
- Meaning
- Integrity
- Continuous growth in knowledge and practice

# Part 4: Practical Tips for Creating
# a Fulfilling Marriage

1. **Visualize yourself as a happily married person.**
   Believe that you are worthy of, deserve, and will achieve a good marriage, and make it a point to interact with people who support these beliefs. Your positive, confident attitude will attract marriage-minded men to you.

2. **Think about why you want to get married.**
   Common Reasons Given for Marrying:
   - So we can live together
   - So we can have children
   - So I won't be lonely
   - To make a substantial commitment
   - To make our relationship official
   - For financial reasons (tax savings, insurance benefits)

   The best reason to marry: Marriage completes us and brings meaning into our lives. In a good marriage, two become one in a miraculous, paradoxical-sounding way that allows each partner to grow and become more than they were before while still maintaining their individuality.

3. **Thinking through some aspects of the kind of marriage you'd like to create:**
   - How will you handle conflicts (different levels or kinds of religious observance, relationships with in-laws or friends, different desires for space versus intimacy, etc.) that may arise?
   - Visualize how you and your future husband will handle details of daily living. During a quiet time alone, imagine and

write down your vision of married life on a typical day. What will you appreciate about each other? How will you handle chores (who cooks, cleans, washes dishes, empties garbage, etc.) and money (who earns it, what's shared/separate)?

- What types of enjoyable activities will you engage in, as a couple and individually, to recharge your batteries and keep the spark alive between the two of you?

- In casual conversations, learn if you and he have a shared vision about marriage.

- Once you are married, or perhaps while engaged, do you want to hold weekly marriage meetings to keep your relationship on track? (See Marriage Meetings, page 88.) They are gentle conversations that foster mutual appreciation, teamwork, and smoother resolutions of issues. Productive marriage meetings keep the spark alive!

## Part 5: Your Action Plan

1. _____
_____
_____
_____

2. _____
_____
_____
_____

3. _____
_____
_____
_____

# Reading List

Allen, Patricia, and Sandra Harmon. *Getting to "I Do": The Secret to Doing Relationships Right!* New York: William Morrow Paperbacks, 1995.

Berger, Marcia Naomi. *Marriage Meetings for Lasting Love: 30 Minutes a Week to the Relationship You've Always Wanted.* Novato, CA: New World Library, 2014.

Berman, Claire. *Adult Children of Divorce Speak Out: About Growing Up With—and Moving Beyond—Parental Divorce.* New York: Simon and Schuster, 1991.

Bloom, Linda, and Charlie Bloom. *101 Things I Wish I Knew When I Got Married: Simple Lessons to Make Love Last.* Novato, CA: New World Library, 2004.

Boteach, Shmuley. *Kosher Sex: A Recipe for Passion and Intimacy.* New York: Doubleday, 1999.

Brizendine, Louann. *The Female Brain.* New York: Broadway Books, 2007.

———. *The Male Brain.* New York: Broadway Books, 2010.

Butler, Pamela. *Self-Assertion for Women.* San Francisco: Harper Collins, 1992.

———. *Talking to Yourself: How Cognitive Behavior Therapy Can Change Your Life.* Charleston, SC: BookSurge, 2008.

Cameron, Julia. *The Artist's Way*. New York: Jeremy P. Tarcher/ Putnam, 1992.

Carlson, Jon, and Don Dinkmeyer. *Time for a Better Marriage: Training in Marriage Enrichment*. Rev. ed. Atascadero, CA: Impact, 2002.

Carter, Steven, and Julia Sokol. *He's Scared, She's Scared: Understanding the Hidden Fears That Sabotage Your Relationship*. New York: Dell, 1995.

Chapman, Gary. *The 5 Love Languages: The Secret to Love That Lasts*. Chicago: Northfield, 2009.

Feldman, Aharon. *The River, the Kettle, and the Bird: A Torah Guide to Successful Marriage*. Spring Valley, NY: Feldheim, 1987.

Gottman, John, and Julie Schwartz Gottman. *Eight Dates: Essential Conversations for a Lifetime of Love*. Ill. ed. New York: Workman Publishing Company, 2019.

Gottman, John, and Nan Silver. *The Seven Principles for Making Marriage Work*. Rev. ed. New York: Harmony, 2015.

Hendrix, Harville, and Helen LaKelly Hunt. *Getting the Love You Want: A Guide for Couples*. Rev. ed. New York: St. Martin's Griffin, 2019.

Johnson, Sue. *Hold Me Tight: Seven Conversations for a Lifetime of Love*. New York: Little, Brown, 2008.

Kreidman, Ellen. *Light His Fire: How to Keep Your Man Passionately and Hopelessly in Love with You*. New York: Dell, 1992.

Page, Susan. *If I'm So Wonderful, Why Am I Still Single? Ten Strategies That Will Change Your Love Life Forever*. Rev. ed. New York: Harmony, 2002.

Price, Deborah. *The Heart of Money: A Couple's Guide to Creating True Financial Intimacy*. Novato, CA: New World Library, 2012.

Taitz, Jennifer. *How to Be Single and Happy: Science-Based Strategies for Keeping Your Sanity While Looking for a Soul Mate*. Ill. ed. New York: TarcherPerigee, 2018.

Walkup, Jim. *I Do! A Marriage Workbook for Engaged Couples*. Workbook edition. San Antonio, TX: Althea Press, 2019.

# Notes

## B

1. Chart and exercise based on presentation by Roland F. Williams, MA, at the Summit for Clinical Excellence in 2003.

## C

1. "Does Love At First Sight Mean Happily Ever After?," Your Tango, posted March 18, 2012, https://www.yourtango.com /experts/nina-atwood/how-fast-do-you-fall-love. This article cites a thirteen-year longitudinal study by Tom Huston at the University of Texas at Austin (Huston et al., 2001).

2. Nagesh Belludi, "Albert Mehrabian's 7-38-55 Rule of Personal Communication," Right Attitudes, posted October 4, 2008, https://www.rightattitudes.com/2008/10/04/7-38-55-rule -personal-communication/.

3. "The Most Underrated Emotion That Can Drive Your Success," Covisioning, posted February 27, 2016, https://covisioning. com/the-most-underrated-emotion-that-can-drive-your -success-curiosity/.

# E

1. Philip Fauerbach, "Communication Conflict: Why Men Want to Fix What Women Just Want Listened To," South Brandon Center for Couples, Anxiety and Trauma, posted April 4, 2016, https://pfauerbachtherapy.com/communication-conflict -men-want-fix-women-just-want-listened/.

# F

1. Anna Hodgekiss, "It's not all about sex: FRIENDSHIP is the secret to a long-lasting romantic relationship," *The Daily Mail*, updated January 28, 2013, https://www.dailymail.co.uk /health/article-2269657/Friendship-sex-secret-long-lasting -romantic-relationship.html.

2. Hanna Kozlowska, "Definitive proof that a good marriage, especially to your best friend, makes you happier," Quartz, updated January 8, 2015, https://qz.com/323172/definitive -proof-that-a-good-marriage-especially-to-your-best-friend -makes-you-happier/.

3. Ibid.

4. Anna Hodgekiss, "It's not all about sex: FRIENDSHIP is the secret to a long-lasting romantic relationship," *The Daily Mail*, updated January 28, 2013, https://www.dailymail.co.uk /health/article-2269657/Friendship-sex-secret-long-lasting -romantic-relationship.html.

# G

1. "Gumption," Cambridge Dictionary, https://dictionary .cambridge.org/us/dictionary/english/gumption.

# H

1. Sharon Jayson, "Hooking up to getting hitched: Yes, it can happen," *The Washington Post*, updated August 19, 2014, https://www.washingtonpost.com/national/religion/hooking-up-to-getting-hitched-yes-it-can-happen/2014/08/19/14626422-27be-11e4-8b10-7db129976abb_story.html.

2. The Pirkei Avos Treasury, *Ethics of the Fathers: The Sages' Guide to Living* (Brooklyn: Mesorah Publications, LTD, 2000), 209–11.

# I

1. Marcia Naomi Berger, *Marriage Meetings for Lasting Love* (Novato, CA: New World Library, 2014). Reprinted with permission.

2. https://www.dictionary.com/browse/no-man-is-an-island. *The New Dictionary of Cultural Literacy,* Third Edition. Copyright © 2005 by Houghton Mifflin Harcourt Publishing Company. Published by Houghton Mifflin Harcourt Publishing Company. All rights reserved.

# J

1. *Marriage Meetings for Lasting Love: 30 Minutes a Week to the Relationship You've Always Wanted* tells, step by step, how partners can hold a weekly gentle conversation that keeps them reconnecting frequently. Marriage meetings foster more romance, intimacy, teamwork, and smoother resolution of issues.

2. Marcia Naomi Berger, *Marriage Meetings for Lasting Love* (Novato, CA: New World Library, 2014). Reprinted with permission.

# L

1. Rabbi Menachem M. Schneerson, Uri Kaplous, and Eliyahu Touger, *Tackling Life's Tasks: Every Day Energized with HaYom Yom* (New York: Sichos, 2010), 98.

2. Joseph Telushkin, *Rebbe: The Life and Teachings of Menachem M. Schneerson, the Most Influential Rabbi in Modern History* (New York: HarperCollins, 2014), 65.

3. Ibid.

# M

1. D.L. Thompson, "Estelle Reiner, Carl Reiner's Wife: 5 Fast Facts You Need to Know," Heavy, updated June 30, 2020, https://heavy.com/entertainment/2020/06/estelle-reiner-carl-reiner-wife/.

2. Nagesh Belludi, "Albert Mehrabian's 7-38-55 Rule of Personal Communication," Right Attitudes, posted October 4, 2008, https://www.rightattitudes.com/2008/10/04/7-38-55-rule-personal-communication/.

3. Rachel Cruze, "Money Ruining Marriages in America," Ramsey Solutions, February 7, 2018, https://www.daveramsey.com/pr/money-ruining-marriages-in-america.

# N

1. For step-by-step details for how to hold successful marriage meetings, see *Marriage Meetings for Lasting Love: 30 Minutes a Week to the Relationship You've Always Wanted*.

# O

1. Jason Koebler, "Study: A Third of New Marriages Began with Online Meetings," *U.S. News & World Report*, posted June 3,

2013, https://www.usnews.com/news/articles/2013/06/03
/study-a-third-of-new-marriages-began-with-online-meetings.

2. Matthew D. Johnson, "No, opposites do not attract," The Conversation, updated February 12, 2018, https://theconversation
.com/no-opposites-do-not-attract-88839.

3. Utpal Dholakia, PhD, "Why Are So Many Indian Arranged
Marriages Successful?," *Pyschology Today*, posted November
24, 2015, https://www.psychologytoday.com/us/blog/the
-science-behind-behavior/201511/why-are-so-many-indian
-arranged-marriages-successful.

4. Eric Barker, "Are arranged marriages happier?," Barking up
the Wrong Tree, posted December 23, 2011, https://www
.bakadesuyo.com/2011/12/are-arranged-marriages-happier/.
Note that partners in these arranged marriages are able to
choose whether or not to marry the recommended person.

5. John M. Gottman, *The Seven Principles for Making Marriage
Work (New York: Three Rivers Press, 1999).*

**P**

1. Tara Parker-Pope, "The Decisive Marriage," *The New York
Times*, posted August 25, 2014, https://well.blogs.nytimes.
com/2014/08/25/the-decisive-marriage/.

**R**

1. Rabbi Nosson Scherman, *The Stone Edition of the Chumash:
The Torah, Haftaros, and Five Megillos with a Commentary
Anthologized from the Rabbinic Writings* (New York: Mesorah
Publications, 1998), 2.

2. David O'Reilly, "When You Say You Believe in God, What Do You Mean?," *Trust* magazine, November 2, 2018, https://www.pewtrusts.org/en/trust/archive/fall-2018/when-you-say-you-believe-in-god-what-do-you-mean.

3. Ellie Lisitsa, "The Four Horsemen: Criticism, Contempt, Defensiveness, and Stonewalling," The Gottman Institute, posted April 23, 2013, https://www.gottman.com/blog/the-four-horsemen-recognizing-criticism-contempt-defensiveness-and-stonewalling/.

## S

1. "Serendipity," *Merriam-Webster.com Dictionary*, Merriam-Webster, https://www.merriam-webster.com/dictionary/serendipity.

2. "Divine providence," Wikipedia, updated December 10, 2020, https://en.wikipedia.org/wiki/Divine_providence.

3. Sheryl Kingsberg, PhD, "Brain Is a Sexual Organ," Healthy Women, posted November 23, 2011, https://www.healthywomen.org/content/ask-expert/7789/brain-sexual-organ.

4. Bill Hendrick, "Benefits in Delaying Sex Until Marriage," WebMD, posted December 28, 2010, https://www.webmd.com/sex-relationships/news/20101227/theres-benefits-in-delaying-sex-until-marriage#1.

5. Ibid.

6. Ezriel Gelbfish, "Study on Arranged Marriages Reveals that Orthodox Jews May Have It Right," The Algemeiner, posted on July 6, 2012, https://www.algemeiner.com/2012/07/06/study-on-arranged-marriages-reveals-that-orthodox-jews-may-have-it-right/.

7. Ibid.

8. Ibid.

9. Emily Esfahani Smith and Galena Rhodes, "In Relationships, Be Deliberate," *The Atlantic*, August 19, 2014, https://www.theatlantic.com/health/archive/2014/08/in-relationships-be-deliberate/378713/.

10. Ibid.

11. "Spontaneity," *Merriam-Webster.com Dictionary*, Merriam-Webster, https://www.merriam-webster.com/dictionary/spontaneity.

## T

1. Danielle Brennan, "4 signs that a man's ready for marriage—and 4 that he's not," *Today*, updated May 17, 2016, https://www.today.com/health/4-signs-man-s-ready-marriage-4-hesnot-t78711.

## X

1. Ellen Kreidman, *Light His Fire/ Light Her Fire: A Program for Men and Women* (Helotes, TX: Mega Systems, 1995).

## Z

1. Jewish wedding ceremonies are traditionally held outdoors under a chuppah, a nuptial canopy that creates a temporary sanctified space for the bride and groom. The chuppah is made of cloth and is supported by four columns.

# Appendix

1. Thanks are due to Rabbi Ahron Hecht of the Richmond Torah Center in San Francisco for much of the "How to Date"

information presented in his *Love and Marriage* seminar in San Francisco, 2008.

2. Based on a presentation by Roland F. Williams, MA, at the Summit for Clinical Excellence in 2003.

# Index

# Acknowledgments

*M*arriage Minded* is about creating a fulfilling relationship with a spouse, yet many of its ideas apply to other relationships. I treasure my relationships with everyone who generously contributed encouragement, feedback, or technical assistance toward this book's making.

These people include Jacqueline Bradley, Adrian Fried, Netty Kahan, Maryan Karwan, Hinda Langer, Adam Maltby, Cecile Noland, Mary Plescia, David Robbins, Dorie Rosenberg, Marian Sanders, Katharine Sands, Ruth Schuler, Arlen Serber, Natalie Schrik, Joyce Steinfeld, Ara Toomians, and Katie Yanow.

A huge thank-you goes to my manuscript readers for your time, conscientiousness, and valuable insights: Ori Benoni, Linda Bloom, David Berger, Francine Falk-Allen, Gloria Finkelstein, Helene King, Leslie Marks, and Marilyn Neugarten.

She Writes Press founder and editorial manager Brooke Warner is a dynamo and a pleasure to work with. I appreciate her for moving me toward decisive action via her clarity, wisdom, and extensive knowledge of virtually all publishing business aspects. I also value Shannon Green, project manager, for her ongoing support, patience, and scheduling. Thank you both.

I appreciate Francis Kelly's impressive editing and Erica Dallman's charming illustrations, showing that a picture is worth at least a thousand words. I'm grateful to people who may not know that their responses and questions contributed to *Marriage Minded*. Reactions like these inspired me to think through my choices:

Some liked the book being addressed to women; others wished it were for both sexes. One man questioned using the A to Z format, but that didn't change my mind. I wanted this book to evoke the clarity and lightheartedness of a primer for young children. A married acquisitions editor said she didn't know any single women over fifty who wanted to get married. Yet a literary agent, a single woman in her late fifties, saw a crying need for a book for women over fifty because "dating is so different for millennials."

All these responses helped me clarify my thoughts for dealing with various aspects of creating *Marriage Minded*.

What good is a book without readers? I appreciate you for reading *Marriage Minded* and for putting its suggestions into practice. In case you're wondering about the A to Z format, it evolved from my desire to keep things simple yet thorough and because I enjoy word games. It's been fun free-associating to come up with entry titles for each letter.

Finally, words cannot express my appreciation for my husband, David Berger, for his unwavering support for my writing and for sharing my commitment every day to creating a lifelong, fulfilling marriage together.

# About the Author

**M**arcia Naomi Berger (née Fisch), MSW, LCSW, leads dynamic marriage and communication workshops and is a popular speaker at conferences. In addition to working as a clinical social worker with a private psychotherapy practice in San Rafael, California, she's taught continuing education classes for therapists at the University of California Berkeley Extension, Alliant International University, and online and in person for various professional associations. While employed by the City and County of San Francisco, she held senior-level positions in child welfare, alcoholism treatment, and psychiatry. She also served as a lecturer on the clinical faculty at the University of California, School of Medicine, and as executive director of Jewish Family and Children's Services of the East Bay. Berger lives in Marin County, California, with her husband, David Berger. She gives their weekly marriage meetings major credit for their lasting happiness together, which inspired her to write her first book, *Marriage Meetings for Lasting Love: 30 Minutes a Week to the Relationship You've Always Wanted.* She may be contacted at mnaomiberger@gmail.com or via books.marcianaomiberger.com.

*Author photo © Patty Spinks*